MY GOD AND I

Other Books by Lewis Smedes

The Incarnation in Modern Anglo-Catholic Theology

All Things Made New

Love Within Limits

Sex for Christians

Mere Morality

*How Can It Be All Right When Everything
  Is All Wrong?*

Forgive and Forget

Caring and Commitment

Choices: Making Hard Decisions in a Complex World

A Life of Distinction

The Art of Forgiving

Shame and Grace

Keeping Hope Alive

MY GOD AND I

A Spiritual Memoir

Lewis B. Smedes

William B. Eerdmans Publishing Company
Grand Rapids, Michigan / Cambridge, U.K.

Wm. B. Eerdmans Publishing Co.
255 Jefferson Ave. S.E., Grand Rapids, Michigan 49503 /
P.O. Box 163, Cambridge CB3 9PU U.K.

Printed in the United States of America

08 07 06 05 04 03   7 6 5 4 3 2 1

ISBN 0-8028-2213-4

www.eerdmans.com

To
   the memory of
      Tjitske and Wytse
      and
         Renske and Melle

Letter to Lew Smedes about God's Presence

by Rod Jellema

I have to look for cracks and crevices.
Don't tell me how God's mercy
is as wide as the ocean, as deep as the sea.
I already believe it, but that infinite prospect
gets farther away the more we mouth it.
I thank you for lamenting his absences —
his absence from marriages going mad,
our sons dying young, from the inescapable
terrors of history: Treblinka. Vietnam.
September Eleven. His visible absence
makes it hard for us in our time
to celebrate his invisible Presence.

This must be why mystics and poets record
the slender incursions of splintered light,
echoes, fragments, odd words and phrases
like flashes through darkened hallways.
These stabs remind me that the proud
portly old church is really only
that cut green slip grafted into a tiny nick
that merciful God himself slit into the stem
of his chosen Judah. The thin and tenuous
thread we hang by, so astonishing,
is the metaphor I need at the shoreline
of all those immeasurable oceans of love.

Contents

A Publisher's Tribute

"Lew," I complained in an e-mail to him about the manuscript for this spiritual memoir, "you've got to quit sending in revisions, or we'll spend the rest of the month collating and never get to the editing."

Lew cared about his prose. In fact, Lew was what editors call a nuisance! He was also thereby what every writer worth his salt must be and what every editor worth her salt deeply loves. Lew was the real thing as a writer, with all the writer's proper anxieties. He knew the writer's dark night of the soul when the only light in the room is the computer screen, glowing desolate and empty. He knew the fear of never finding the right word or the right way into a paragraph — or worse, of having blundered onto the wrong path never to get out of the woods again. He knew, too — as we his readers later came to know — the ecstasy of the sentence that somehow, mysteriously and as a gift, did turn out right. If on occasion the Smedesian prose got imagistically and otherwise a little out of hand — and Lew, especially in the early days, made his fair share of contributions to the Eerdmans fun drawer of editorial outtakes — well, that was the price to be paid to the creative impulse and to the highly associative mind. No soaring flights without the occasional calamitous plunge into the thicket of mixed metaphors.

But of course style is mere artifice and no style at all without substance, and Lew the writer had substance. In fact, this is where the real wrestling went on: Lew struggling hard — so very hard — to be true to his subject and to its intractable difficulties. He came at his task with a splendid mind splendidly schooled by the likes of G. C. Berkouwer and Karl Barth and his beloved Henry Stob. He also came at his task from a tradition. The trouble with a lot of people, the writer Flannery O'Connor once said, is that they "ain't *frum* anywhere." Lew was. You can read in this memoir about his Frisian grandparents, Wytse and Tjitske Benedictus, one Mennonite and one Reformed. You can read as well about how Jakie Vandenbosch of the Calvin College English department sold the young Lew on the beauties of Calvinism by championing a God who so affirmed his creation that he cared intensely about the well-being of the English sentence. "Jacob Vandenbosch," says Lew, "introduced me . . . to a God the likes of whom I had never even heard about — a God who liked elegant sentences and was offended by dangling modifiers. . . . I found the joy of the Lord, not at a prayer meeting, but in English Composition 101." Not that Lew always *liked* where he came from, but it gave him much of the raw material of his work and it gave him many of the critical tools with which to do that work.

Of course, whatever the importance of ideas and principles (explored in their more theoretical aspect in books like *Mere Morality* and *Love Within Limits*), there was, as Lew himself might have put it, deep in the grip of alliteration, the "stark, stiff stuff" of everyday reality. "The theologian and philosopher," he once wrote, "can all too easily appear to be wrestling hard with moral issues, all the while ignoring real persons caught up in the moral ambiguities of human existence." This surely was at the center of Lew's genius as a writer — and as a teacher, preacher, and pastor. If his address to the issues of real life could never ignore hard and disciplined thinking about principles, neither could it avert its gaze from the hard cases (which, as Lew showed with such meticulous care, so many cases are) and from the human pain in which they are imbedded. This is what made books like *Forgive and Forget* and *Standing on the Promises* speak so convincingly and helpfully to a wide audience of readers. Lew's mind never strayed far from his heart, and his supreme gift was that he did not attend to one and then to the other, but that the two concerns were so seamlessly and authentically woven together and of a piece.

It is no surprise that Lew's empathy for the hurts and struggles of others had everything to do with his own human pain and uncertainties. The man who taught others to hope knew firsthand of what he spoke—or struggled to speak. *How Can It Be All Right When Everything Is All Wrong?* he titled perhaps his most anguished book, written after the death of one of his dearest friends. And at the end of the day, of course, his deepest questions were for his God, the joy of whose presence he amply knew, but whom, Jacob-like, he also could not let off the hook in the dead of the night. Still, as Lew testifies at the close of this memoir, the issue was ultimately the other way around: it was God who would not let him go. "It has been 'God and I' the whole way," says Lew. "Not so much because he has always been pleasant company. Not because I could always feel his presence when I got up in the morning or when I was afraid to sleep at night. It was because he did not trust me to travel alone."

Lew did genially answer my protesting e-mail. Yes, he said, he would quit sending revisions to the manuscript — and wait to tinker more until the proofs! It was his last note to me. Lew Smedes died suddenly and unexpectedly on December 19, 2002, of complications from a serious fall. My last note to him had been only one word. "Thanks." How little could I know how much meaning that word would have to bear. Even so, then, Lewis Benedictus Smedes, colleague, mentor . . . nuisance . . . friend. Thanks.

— *Jon Pott*

Acknowledgments

I must make known my thanks to some dear friends and relatives who, in their special ways, helped me to write this book.

The stories of Beppe Tjitske and Pake Wytse come from my mother's older sister Jeltje, whom Doris and I came to know while we were students in Amsterdam many years ago, and from my mother's younger sister Anna, who told them to her children, one of whom, her son-in-law Daniel Vriend, faithfully wrote them all down. And, of course, from my own mother, who recalled her life with my father in a memorable taped conversation with two of her grand-sons, Paul and Donald Trap. My sister Jessie and brother Peter helped with their childhood memories of my father.

After I had finished a reasonably good draft, I began to have doubts about the decency of publishing a book that was so much about myself. Doris was, as she has been for all of our fifty-four years together, both an honest critic and a convincing encourager. She persuaded me that the book was not really about me at all; that the snippets that I tell about my own life only create a setting for my story of God. I then sent a copy to a few honest friends, Alvin Hoksbergen, George Stob, and John Suk, and asked them to read it and advise me; they all thought it should be published. I am specially thankful to Maryland's wonderful poet, Roderick Jellema, for honoring me by reading the manuscript and giving me unfailingly helpful suggestions. These people all persuaded me to publish in spite of my personal misgivings, but my decision to publish came, in the end, from my own growing conviction that I owed my church and the readers of my other books an account of my life with God. ✢

Preface

As I neared retirement almost a decade ago, I had but one project in mind for myself, getting the fundamentals of my faith in clearer focus. There are some things about God that, were I to stop believing them, my world would change color, my hope would turn sour, and the meaning of my life would be yanked inside out. But I believe other things about God that, were I to stop believing them, would not undermine my faith, would not dim my hope, and would not change the meaning of my life. So I set out to separate the theological opinions that I hold — or that I doubt — from the faith that I live by.

Before I had gotten very far, I began to feel that I owed some people a progress report. I owed it to people who have read my books for instance; most of my books have not been expressly about God but about human life and how it can and should be lived. I also owed it to my brothers and sisters in the community of faith to which I belong; they care about and have a right to know what their teachers and preachers think and believe about God. So I decided to write a small book that I was going to call *Brass Tacks — The Nonnegotiables* of my faith.

I was busy with this project when a dear friend sent me a postcard with a message he said was from the Lord. The message was that I should drop whatever intellectual work I was doing and write my memoir instead. I have much respect for my friend's ability to recognize God's signals when he gets them, but I was sure that he had been misled on this one. Both God and I would blush at my presumption.

But then I began to wonder. Could I write a book that would be neither a memoir nor a theology, but a combination of the two? What if I told certain parts of my story, not because they would be, in themselves, interesting, but as settings for my thoughts about and my experiences with God? The snippets from my life story would be like a collection of snapshots rather than a penned biography. The snapshots would provide the setting for what I was thinking and experiencing of God at the time they were taken. This, then, is how this little book turned out to be, neither a collection of essays about God nor a story of my life, but an account of my doubts and my pains, my faith and my hope as I walked with my elusive God down the winding trail from there to here.

I am only giving my testimony, or a confession of some sort, no more than that. I have no desire to change anybody's mind or challenge anybody's faith. Some readers may think that this account of my travel with God is too trivial to bother with and my thoughts of God too wrongheaded to be worth arguing with. That would be fine with me. All I ask from them is trust that I have tried to be honest with them, and honest to God in the bargain.

CHAPTER ONE

Beppe Tjitske

M y grandfather, my Pake, on my mother's side, was Wytse Benedictus, a peat farmer and a Mennonite. He lived near a small village called Rottevalle, which lies in the center of Friesland, the northernmost province of the Netherlands. While Friesland is indeed a province and not a country, its people know that they are a race and culture apart, with their own language and their own history, the fiercest warriors of all the Gauls, according to Julius Caesar, who knew what he was talking about. But since then, according to Baedecker, the travel guide man, they have produced nothing more interesting than an uncommon lot of schoolteachers; he said it in mild derision, but most Frisians would have taken it as a fine tribute. It was here that the forebears of the Frisian Mennonites had settled after their flight from persecution by the Swiss Reformers.

The Benedictus family had been Mennonites from before the time the Mennonites named their movement after the converted priest Menno Simons, the greatest of their leaders. They were a peaceable people, these Mennonites, radical children of the Protestant Reformation whom the Calvinists and Lutherans contemptuously called Anabaptists (*ana* being the equivalent of "again") because they baptized adult converts by immersion even though they had already, as newborn babies, been baptized by sprinkling in the Reformed Church.

The Swiss Calvinists, in the words of a contemporary wag, figured that if these Anabaptists wanted so badly to be immersed, the Reformers would accommodate them by drowning them.

By the seventeenth century, the Mennonites in Friesland had begun to prosper, mostly because the land was ripe with peat, which was used as fuel and sold mainly to Germany. By the early sixteen hundreds, the Benedictus family had become wealthy owners of a considerable peat estate and by 1620 had built a modest manor on it. Pake Wytse is in his early forties — the year being uncertain, but sometime in the early 1880's — when we come upon him in the Benedictus manor, unmarried and apparently destined to remain so, a man highly regarded among the faithful for both his Christian character and his worldly goods.

Not far from the Benedictus estate, in a hovel near Rottevalle, lived a dirt-poor Frisian by the name of Reinder van der Bij, not blessed with any land but well cursed with many daughters — seven of them. Reinder could see no future in daughters, certainly not in seven of them, so, as most serfs in his circumstance did, he shipped all but the oldest out to work as virtual slaves on richer people's farms. One of the sisters was my grandmother Tjitske, who was sent off at age twelve or thirteen.

For Tjitske's fourteen hours of daily labor she earned two and half guilders (roughly four dollars) per year as a supplement to the food she consumed and the space in the barn that she occupied. She served one farmer until she was nineteen, when she was seduced and made pregnant by a roving carpenter. As soon as her belly betrayed her condition, she was pointed to her master's door and told to carry her baby along with her shame back to her father and home.

Reinder van der Bij, however, was not a man to be publicly shamed by a harlot daughter, and so, with a proper Old Testament curse, he sent her packing. No other Frisian man was likely to open his door to a fallen woman, and she took to begging in the streets. Her weeks or months on the streets are blacked out; we know nothing of her until she is rescued by Wytse and installed as a servant in the Benedictus manor. However she came to the manor, Wytse provided her a place to care for her newborn daughter and then left her on her own to keep house in a manner proper for a pure-of-heart Mennonite bachelor.

Sometime after he took her in from the streets, Wytse discovered that she could be of even more help to him in business than she was as a housekeeper. The trade in peat was carried on by spoken words, a handshake, and an exchange of cash. It was the spoken-words part that gave Wytse trouble. He stuttered. He stuttered even more than usual when he had a deal to make. So he was not offended when the servant girl he had taken in off the street offered to help him.

"Why don't you write your words down and let me speak them for you?" she asked.

Good idea, he said, and so it was that the two of them became working partners. Wytse swiftly became dependent on Tjitske, who gradually took over the peat negotiations as well as the management of the manor. Their working partnership flowered into personal attachment, and on the 26th of July in the year 1884, Wytse and Tjitske — destined now to be my grandmother, my Beppe Tjitske — were married. Both the Calvinists and the Mennonites assumed that the obedient bride would convert to the religion of her benefactor husband. But it was Wytse who pulled up his Mennonite roots and replanted them in his bride's Reformed faith.

Wytse knew the Mennonites well. A single Mennonite would never raise his hand against anyone, but a community of Mennonites could make a person's life miserable simply by ignoring her. So Pake Wytse and Beppe Tjitske left the Benedictus manor in the hands of a caretaker and moved into a smaller and rougher farm house that Wytse owned at the edge of a Protestant village called Ureterp, where their graves are still marked. Here the couple created a family of six children. Renske, the third born, would one day, in another world, give birth to me.

When we pick up the story again, Pake Wytse was sixty-four and, on this particular day, was ice skating, probably on a canal that edged the farm. He fell and broke his hip. He did not mend; he got rapidly worse, and he died, in agony it is said, within a few weeks of his fall. The widow Tjitske, braving Mennonite rejection, moved her seven children back to the great house in Rottevalle. She inherited all of Wytse's assets, land and cash, and managed them as well as she was able.

Being lady of the manor and manager of the peat farm was, however, a tough task for a novice widow with seven children. But an offer of help came soon in the guise of a charming widower named Wiebe Geksma. Wiebe, who posed as a man with the most honorable intentions and with money enough to care for both their families, offered himself to Tjitske, and Tjitske took him in. Wiebe promised to take care of her and seek her happiness, so they were soon married.

Wiebe waited no more than a few months after the wedding to show his hand. He told Tjitske that, since he was now the head of both the house and the wife, it was her duty to transfer the entire estate to him. Tjitske balked; the money was meant for Wytse's children, she said, and only his children were going to get it. Wiebe then tore the cover of charm off his pathology and his demons flew free. The children were his first victims, especially the girls; the boys he terrorized, the girls he assaulted. My future mother, the teenage Renske, was, I learned many years later, his favorite victim.

Wiebe tyrannized Beppe's family until, one Frisian winter night, he went one step too far: he threw Beppe Tjitske and her children out in the cold. When morning came, she went to the village police and begged them to come and rescue her brood. They went, evicted Wiebe and his children, and provided the Benedictus family with police protection. Tjitske obtained a legal separation and, soon afterward, spurning the shame of both the Mennonite and the Reformed camps, arranged for a divorce.

The Benedictus manor was, like all things Frisian, plain and rough. Barn and house were under one thatched roof, separated by a kitchen door that hung in two sections so that the woman of the house could open the upper half, speak to laborers and yell at the animals, while the lower half stayed locked against invasion by livestock. One Sunday morning at Beppe Tjitske's Reformed church, with the dominie well into his sermon and the congregation already smelling their Lord's Day coffee, the custodian rushed into the sanctuary yelling: *Vuur bij Benedictus!!* Fire at Benedictus — words dreaded by every farmer more than a prognosis of his own imminent death. And words that emptied any packed church in two minutes flat.

By the time the men of the congregation could get to the

farm, the entire building, house and barn and every living thing in it, was aflame. The next day the villagers came with butchers' knives to slice off prodigious chunks of barbequed pork and beef, enough to provide them with a month of feasting. The ancient manor was gone.

Meanwhile, Beppe Tjitske's single source of income dwindled as coal began to replace peat for use as fuel in Europe. To make matters sadder, her first daughter, the carpenter's child, had married, and her husband had swindled Beppe out of a large amount of cash. So by the time the manor burned, the Benedictus estate had already been drained.

My mother Renske had by this time sailed off to America with her new husband, Melle Smedes, a village blacksmith, the son of generations of blacksmiths before him. In 1932, Beppe Tjitske died a few minutes after whispering her favorite verses from her favorite psalm:

The Lord preserveth the simple:
I was brought low, and he helped me.
Thou hast delivered my soul from death,
Mine eyes from tears,
My feet from falling.   (Psalm 116:6, 8)

Later, a money-order for two hundred dollars signed to my mother came in the mail from Rottevalle, and the last of Beppe Tjitske's modest fortune was spent to pay for a new roof over a new set of Frisian heads at 774 Amity Street in Muskegon, Michigan.

I think of Beppe Tjitske's and Pake Wytse's mixed marriage, a rare and suspect thing in their time and place, as a parable of the religious mix in my own spirit. I like both ingredients in the mix. I like the tough intellectual side of the Reformed faith. And I like the gentle affections of the Mennonite faith. I share the Reformed wariness of radical piety. I share the Mennonite suspicion of rigid dogmatism. ✣

CHAPTER TWO

Melle Smedes

My father's Frisian name was Melle and the name-changers at Ellis Island let it stay that way. He built our house on Amity Street in Muskegon during the fading hours of daylight after he came home from his nine- or ten-hour shift at the foundry. He had never built anything before; the only use he had ever put a hammer to was nailing shoes to horses' hooves.

The front porch of the house he built for us was studded with pink and white Kelly stones, which, I always felt, gave it a touch of distinction in our plain neighborhood. The porch was almost as wide as the house and deep enough to hold the army surplus cot that my brother Peter had found at the junkyard where he scavenged regularly for stray items that might come in handy around our house. At the other end of the porch was our one conspicuous luxury, a two-person swing hanging uncertainly from hooks in the ceiling.

If we walked straight from the bottom porch step, we

would run smack into the finest maple tree on our maple-lined Amity Street. Its trunk was almost four feet through the middle, and its full-spread branches shaded our entire porch, making it bearable for us to sit on the swing and dream through the hottest of summer afternoons. The few moments that I would spend alone with my mother during the week were on late Sunday afternoons swinging cool in the shadow of our maple and greeting the neighbors finishing up their Sabbath walks; they were the happiest moments of my childhood.

The rest of the house, to be honest about it, was not the work of a craftsman. Window sills and door frames were not plumb, and, except for a flushing toilet, it lacked all the amenities normal for the time. But we did have one luxury in our living room that only a few houses could boast of — a pump organ, the kind that depended on a robust pair of legs to fill the bellows. I do not know how we came to have such an instrument in our house. None of us ever had an urge to learn to play it, and it came to a bad end. My mother decided that it was doing none of us any good and was made of good wood, so, short as we were on kindling for starting our fires, she had us lug the organ down to the basement, where Peter hacked its panels apart and chopped them into slender sticks that got the fire going in the coal stove in whose oven we warmed our feet before putting them into our socks and shoes.

Being but two months old when he died, I have no memories of my father, but he stands handsome on the one or two snapshots my mother saved, a strong angular face, thick black hair, and a Ronald Coleman mustache. My mother did not speak much about him, but more than once I heard him called a rolling stone; he evidently had a penchant for taking on more than he could handle, dropping it, and moving on to his next dream.

My mother used to deplore his initial decision, before Amity Street in Muskegon, to settle the family in a "one-horse town" called Reeman, which had almost enough horses to provide him with one day's work every week. How could he feed his growing family on that? The only other occupation available around Reeman was farming, so he rented a piece of ground, bought two pigs and a few chickens from a land-rich neighbor, and tried farming for a season, keeping the smithy as a sideline. But he was no farmer, and he gave it up. He gave up Reeman, too, and moved his family to Muskegon, a bustling foundry town a morning's wagon ride away. There he worked himself to an early death in a foundry designed to crush the dreams of all who labored there.

My father was not what you would call a practical man. He and my mother had what was supposed to be an untouchable three hundred dollars salted in the bank for a rainy day, a good-by gift from Beppe Tjitske. But, while they still lived in Reeman, he took a shine to an electric automobile — an original O'Henry — owned by an itinerant physician, and when he was given a chance to buy it for three hundred dollars, he hustled off to the bank, took out the family funds, and bought the car.

He loaded his family in for a trip to Grand Rapids, a good forty miles from Reeman, to show their Henry off to another immigrant Frisian family. A few miles out, the engine stalled. So Melle sent Renske to the rear of the car to push until she got tired enough to risk setting her behind the wheel while he got in back to push. With his head pointed downward between his shoulders, his frontward vision was blocked by the car, and he could not see the valley directly ahead of them, nor the downhill track of the dirt road. Renske and the car started coasting down the hill before Melle had a chance to stop it. He yelled at Renske to step on the brakes, but she had no idea of what a brake was or where it was or how she was supposed to step on it. She and the car kept rolling downhill until it veered to the right and ran into a watery ditch.

Melle left the considerably shaken Renske in the car, with the rest of the family, while he walked a mile or so down the road to a farm where he found a man willing to lead a couple of horses back to the car and pull it out of the ditch. The horses, however, were skittish about the strange contraption, and before they agreed to be hitched to it, they kicked at it and left the front end considerably the worse off for their kicks. But once hitched, the horses calmed down and pulled the car up on the road.

Back on the road again, Melle promised his family a happy journey. But if it wasn't one thing it was another, and before they arrived in Grand Rapids, all four tires had blown out. After ten hours on the road, the Smedeses, clattering on four bare rims, arrived at the home of their friends. The next morning Melle found a sucker willing to take the O'Henry in exchange for a tired horse and a worn-out buggy. Melle, however, was as unschooled at driving a buggy as he was at driving a car, and, at one juncture, the horse took over the controls and trotted off at his own initiative across a farmer's field, buggy and Smedeses bumping behind. The nag knocked over the outhouse and let out an offended neigh. The farmer ran out of the house, got hold of the reins, and sent the horse and buggy on its way. Except for this one small bother, Melle brought his family safely home again.

I had heard my mother talk of how Melle wasted his time down in the basement inventing things that never came to anything. Once, passing the time of day at the Hackley Public Library when I was supposed to be at school, I paged through some bound copies of the records of the Patent Office and discovered the patent issued to him by the United States government for a contraption he had invented for lighting up the houses and barns of outback areas of the country. Nothing came of his invention, but my discovery comforted me with a notion that my father would have understood me and my dreaming even if nobody else in my family could. I gave voice to this notion once and my mother took it as a complaint against her.

My older sister Jessie has a few memories of my father and tells one story about him that I especially like. It was nearly Christmas, and she had been enchanted by the evergreen trees with lights and tinsel hanging on their branches that she saw through our neighbors' windows. She wondered where one came by such magical things. My father suggested that the people who had Christmas trees probably had gone into the woods and chopped them down. Now it happened that within walking distance from our house were some fields of scrub brush and, here and there, a struggling baby pine. So Jessie found my father's hatchet and scouted the area for a Christmas tree.

She settled on a beauty, four feet high if an inch, put her hatchet to it, lugged it to our back yard, and wondered what to do with it. If she brought it boldly to our parents, her father might say: "There will be no stolen Christmas tree in this house." Take it back then? Not on her life. So she hid it discreetly in the basement and hoped that her parents would find it, and not knowing where it came from, let her keep it.

But the day before Christmas arrived, and nothing had been said about the tree. When they finished their pea soup supper that night, Melle muttered that he was going to walk over to Lindstrom's drug store to buy his Christmas cigar and that he expected the children to be asleep when he returned.

Christmas day, Jessie awoke early and sneaked into the front room to pinch the packages of newly knit mittens and store-bought underwear that were our standard Christmas presents. Then she saw her tree standing in the corner of the room anchored in a tree stand that my father had made, wound about with red ribbon and dotted with candles. Delirious with happiness, she woke the other children and persuaded my father to light the candles at once, which he did, with solid kitchen matches, the kind a man could light with his finger nail. He lit the first candle, near the top, then the second and third lower down, and, when his match burned too close to his fingers, he lit a fresh one. When he put his thumb nail to the match, its lighted tip flew into a branch and set the tree on fire. Melle with heroic calm threw a carpet over the blaze before it could spoil a fine Christmas day.

When Christmas came to our house the next time, our father had been, at age thirty-three, dead for three months. ✦

CHAPTER THREE

Renske

My mother's real name was Renske, but at Ellis Island they made her change it to Rena. Every comfort I was taught to seek from my heavenly Father I looked for in her, my earthly mother, but, all the time I was growing up, she was working too hard and working too much to have either time or energy to get close to me long enough for me to find God's comfort in her. I was never conscious of missing my missing father whom I had never known, but I missed my mother all too often.

Before my father had a chance to finish the house he was building for us on Amity Street, he dropped back on his bed early one Monday morning and died. So there she was, barely old enough to be called a woman, with neither kith nor kin on the continent. Struck almost mad with grief and terror, she managed somehow to get my father properly buried. But what then?

She spoke only peasant Frisian laced with a few Americanisms that she had picked up from her neighbors. She had no job skills and had never had a penny of her own to manage. Public welfare was still years away, and five mindless kids whined in the kitchen for something to eat. So a few days after she buried her husband, she was out scrubbing rich people's floors on her hands and knees and washing their clothes at home in a secondhand Maytag. Moved to Christian sympathy by her distress, caring neighbors came to our house and counseled her that it was probably the will of God for her to give two or three of her children away.

She was round, a bit on the heavy side, but nobody thought of her as fat; all in all, when she was dressed up she cut a fine figure. One reason she looked slimmer than she was is that she never sagged; as she walked tired and footsore down Amity Street towards home after a long day's work and a two-mile walk, she was still standing straight, shoulders square, head up, as if she were just leaving a tea party at the dominie's house. Her face was well tailored, soft edged but with a firm, serious nose. Her only blemish was a mole on the center of her chin with prickly hair growing out from it that my sisters would take a scissors to every Sunday morning before we all headed to church.

Renske was not a woman given to rational reflection. She responded to her world, to us kids, and to her neighbors almost entirely by feelings, which in her case were almost always generous. Her problem, however, was not that she ran on feeling, it was that she dared not trust her own feelings; she waited for other people to tell her how they felt about things and only then decided how she should feel about them. She loved us dearly, but whenever a neighbor or friend, or even one of her older children, told her something about us that made her feel ashamed of us, she took on the other person's feeling and would, with mournful unction, report it to us.

When I was fifteen she found a copy of *College Humor* under my mattress, a magazine with forbidden pictures of young women in their underwear. They were more fully covered then the women who model lingerie in *The New York Times,* but still, to look was shameful. She dared not trust her own feelings about her discovery, so she asked my oldest brother what he thought about it. Peter, who at the time was fresh from having been born again, told her the worst, which she then dolefully recited to me. "Peter says that you are rotten, Lewis, yes, Lewis, rotten, Peter said so, yes, Lewis, Peter says that you are rotten." She said it once, and to be sure that it had sunk in, she kept pouring it like warm tar over my rotted soul: rotten, rotten, rotten. I am certain now that she did not really believe what Peter had said, if, indeed, he had actually said it. But I believed it and I believed that God believed it too.

My mother felt about work the way a monk feels about prayer. So one way to please her was to find gainful employment outside the house at a bright and early age. I was too young to deliver newspapers at the time, but I could buy newspapers at my own risk for two cents each and hawk them downtown for three cents a paper. Our paper was the *Muskegon Chronicle,* and all the news boys hawked it as if *Chronicle* were spelled *Eernichoal* and sang it as if it were a Gregorian chant.

I had earned the better part of a dollar by Christmastime and went downtown one Saturday morning to buy my mother my first Christmas gift, but I ran into an obstacle in front of Woolworth's five and dime store. A Salvation Army Santa Claus was ringing a bell over a bucket and pleading with shoppers to remember the poor children of the town at this wondrous season. I was, the moment I heard his plea, all but paralyzed with worry about those poor children, but I resisted his call; I closed my eyes and ears and walked right past Santa Claus into Woolworth's. Still, those poor children would not give me any peace. I walked back out of the store and past Santa Claus, turned around, and resisted him again. My resistance got weaker every time I passed him until my spirit softened and allowed me to divide my resources evenly between the poor children and my poor mother.

The only place one could buy a serious Christmas present for fifty cents was the Liquidating Store on Pine street, not quite downtown, a street of shabby stores that once felt right at home with classy establishments like J. C. Penney and F. W. Woolworth. They sold things there that regular stores could not get rid of; Liquidating was where I went.

The best thing I could find on sale there for less than fifty cents was a set of four dull-gray over-sized table spoons at ten cents a piece. I bought them, wrapped them in tissue paper and put them under our tree. When my mother opened the package on Christmas morning in front of my siblings, they looked at my gift with scorn. "Spoons? What kind of dumb gift is that?" And for weeks around our house my name was "Spoons." But my mother said: "Lewis has a good heart," and her defense of my foolish generosity has been a word of grace to me each time it has come back to mind.

Her impulses now and then pushed her into risky solutions to sudden crises. For instance, one morning of a severe winter, my older sister and brother were sitting on the edge of the kitchen table putting their hands and fingers on the fantastic forms that Jack Frost had painted on the window. The table tipped and my sister and brother smashed straight through the window. On hearing the glass shatter and the children scream, Renske sprang through the jagged pieces of glass like a circus lion through a hoop and landed unharmed in five feet of snow. She always did say that God took specially good care of widows and never wondered why a God who cared so much for widows could not have prevented her from becoming one in the first place.

When the Great Depression had gotten a grip on the United States and Franklin Roosevelt had become President, our standard of living was actually ratcheted up by a couple of notches. Getting benefits from Roosevelt's New Deal, however, tested my mother's faith, because her Republican grocer warned her that Roosevelt was probably the Antichrist and that the New Deal was the beginning of the Great Apostasy. Fortunately, her needs overcame her scruples, and she ended up accepting a handout even if it did come from the Antichrist. In fact, better from the government than from the deacons of the church. Once you were enrolled in welfare, the government pretty much left you alone. But the deacons never stopped snooping around to make sure that nobody was eating too high off the hog on the church's charity.

When her impulses pushed her to buy anything that cost more than five dollars, she would tumble head first into a deep ravine of buyer's remorse. I had gotten to be fourteen or fifteen when she bought a secondhand gas stove to replace the fat black coal burner which she had until then used to cook all our meals and heat our kitchen. The most amiable feature of the old coal burner was an oven large enough for all of us at the same time to warm our chilled feet on winter mornings without once wondering who it was that had lugged the coal out of the cellar and got it burning in our stove that early in the morning in the first place. But once the gas stove was hooked up, what with its automatic pilot light and instant heat, we felt as if our stock in life had risen by at least a few points, and we told her how smart she had been to get it so cheap. But for five nights running, she got up from her bed in the middle of the night, sat down in front of it, put her face in her hands, shook her head, and asked God to forgive her for her folly.

My older brothers, Wesley and Peter, paid regular visits to the city junkyard (which I grew up thinking was Potter's Field, where they buried Judas Iscariot) to look for reusable bicycle parts; every bike any of us ever owned was assembled from junkyard castaways. At the same time, they kept their eyes open for anything that might turn out to be usable at our house. One time, Peter dug up a few broken umbrellas, oversized black ones, and laid them at my mother's feet. Good find, she said, and then made three pairs of bloomers out of them, one for herself and the other two for my sisters.

Years later, when she was eighty-six, Renske fell and broke her hip for the second time and was laid up in a hospital just when I happened to be giving some seminars at Hope College, some twenty miles from Muskegon. Since I was occupied at the college only in the morning hours, I had a chance to spend every afternoon with her and we did a lot of talking about things that I wished we had talked about long before.

"Oh Lewis," she said to me at the end of one day, "I'm so glad that the Lord forgives all of my sins, because, you know, I have been a great sinner."

"Great sinner? You never had time to do any real sinning, Mother. Tell me, what sins do you have in mind?"

"Oh Lewis, you must not talk that way; I know that I am a terrible sinner and God forgives me and that's all I can say."

Deep into one afternoon, when we were just about talked out, I had an impulse to ask her something I had often wondered about and never thought it decent to ask. Why had she never gotten married again? "You were so young, only thirty, a good-looking woman, and you must have been awfully lonely. Didn't you ever want a man in your life? A man to take care of you? A man to talk to at the end of a day? A man to sleep with you?"

"Oh yes," she said, "I did; I felt so tired and so alone, and I sometimes wished that I had a husband, but I was afraid that if another man came into the house, he might not care for my children as I did."

I knew then that I had found the love of my heavenly Father tucked into the love of my earthly mother. ✤

CHAPTER FOUR

Sour Hour of Prayer

As the undertakers carried my father's body from our living room where it had been on display for a few days, my mother, I am told, slowly rocked back and forth in a rocking chair with her face buried in her hands and moaned over and over: *God is zoo zuur.* God is so sour. She had wanted to taste the sweetness of God, but had found the taste of him sour to her soul.

The sweet hour of prayer was never sweet at our house. Not for me. Whenever we as a family tried to get personal with God, I wept. Meeting God seemed to be a sadness for my mother, too, which made it doubly sad for me, especially when she showed her sadness at prayer meetings. So when the Sunday evening service at our church was closing down, and our dominie, the Rev. Harry Bultema, summoned us all downstairs to the fellowship hall for the prayer meeting, I knew the hour of sadness had come.

Sitting next to her, I could feel her twisting and rocking at her hips, struggling with her longings to lay her needs before the Lord on the one hand and her fear of shaming herself before the congregation on the other. She always waited to pray until the pauses between other people's prayers got longer and the prayers themselves began to lose their steam. Then she would stand up to pray. In Frisian. I did not know what she was saying, but I could feel her body swaying back and forth, pausing now and then so that she could gulp down sobs and hold back tears. She heaved out her petitions until she could go on no longer and then, before she could get out her Amen, sat herself down and wept.

I wanted to put my head on her lap and bawl with her. I wanted to get away from there and never ever go to a prayer meeting again. Though I have since then gone to a lot of prayer meetings, I cannot remember one to which I went gladly.

There was sadness, too, when I was born again. It happened at Laketon Avenue Mission Sunday School, one of the afternoon supplements to our regular Sunday School lessons. Our own Sunday School was geared to teaching children who were already in the fold; the Mission was geared to save children's souls and bring them into the fold. The teacher of my class was Sid Seaton. Sid played a guitar and a harmonica at the same time, the latter being held in his mouth by a harness around his neck so that he could blow while his fingers strummed his guitar as an accompaniment.

Sid always ended his lesson with time left for us to bow our heads and pray as the Spirit moved us. I knew that if I felt led to pray out loud, I would surely bawl, so I resisted, until Sid asked me personally if I didn't want to lead in prayer like the other kids did. Since he singled me out, I could hardly turn him down. I began to pray, but before I had really gotten into it, I broke down bawling, pretty much the way my mother did. Sid seized the moment: "Would you like to tell us what is on your heart, Lewis?" I had no idea of what was on my heart, but I knew that Sid wanted Jesus to be in my heart, and I could not bear to disappoint him. So I said it, "I've never been born again before, but now I am." Sid broke out in a psalm-like chant: "Praise the Lord, Oh, praise the Lord, Bless his holy name."

I never felt worse. And I knew that this was only the beginning of my sorrow. For Sid would surely share his joy with my brother Wes, and Wes would go home and as soon as he got inside the door would yell out to the family: "Luke got born again." And I knew that they would all think in their hearts: "Yeah? Well, we'll see."

My brother Peter, oldest of us three boys, was really and truly born again; it happened at the Gospel Hall, a ten-minute walk from our house and still another Sunday supplement to our Lord's Day diet. Soon after he was converted, Peter decided that we ought to have family devotions the way other Christian families did. We tried it at night before going to bed; we set the kitchen chairs around in a small circle and waited for each other to offer a prayer. The prayers came slowly. I kept my mouth shut because I had a hunch that I would bawl the moment I exposed my sorry soul to God in the presence of my own family. But after a few nights of family devotions, Peter asked me if I didn't want to say a prayer too. I didn't want to, but I did it anyway, and, as I could have warned them, I broke down and cried. Peter assured me that the Bible said the "tears of his saints were precious in the eyes of the Lord," which did not comfort me much. After a week or so, we gave up on family devotions, and each of us went to bed at our own times and did our praying beneath the blankets.

My mother's prayers were sad, I suppose, because she so deplored the fact that she was an uncommonly bad sinner. But she thanked God for the Lord Jesus who forgave all of her grievous sins. And that kept her going.

Renske was not really what you would call a melancholy woman. She remembered mostly the good times and she laughed a lot about them. It was when God came in that sadness got the better of her. Whenever God was in the air, she wanted to tell him that she felt very bad about not being good enough, not a good enough mother, not a good enough Christian, not smart enough, not refined enough, just plain not good enough at anything.

There was some compensation to her sad feelings. Feeling unworthy of anything very good, she never complained that she did not get much of it. She never asked why she should have been stuck in a strange land with no husband, no money, and with five unreasonable kids; the question of

"Why me?" never seemed to enter her head. She seemed convinced that whatever her lot, it was what had to be and that her job was simply to do as well as she could with what little she was given, never doubting that God has a tender spot in his heart for widows.

The trouble, as far as I was concerned, was that her sense of unworthiness was infectious. Obsessed with her own lack of any virtue worth praising, my mother did not have it in her to persuade us children that there was any virtue in us worth noting either. When friends from our church came to visit and bragged about their children, my mother would complain about hers in a desperate hope that her friends would contradict her, which they never did. Small wonder, I suppose, that as a boy I was thoroughly convinced that God held his nose as he passed me by and if, by chance, he gave me a second look, he had to resist an impulse to turn me into a pillar of salt.

All in all, God seldom wore a happy face in my boyhood and ever since the sadness of God has come more naturally to me than the joy of the Lord. Even now I hardly dare sing all stanzas of *Just As I Am* because chances are that I will break down and weep if I do.

Since this chapter has been about my childhood affairs with prayer it may be as good a place as any to admit that even my grown-up prayers are a mystery to me. I pray a lot, but never for long stretches at a time; I am just not able to concentrate on God for more than ten minutes. And yet some people think that my prayers are unusually efficacious. Recently a rabbi drove forty miles from his home to mine only because he wanted me to pray for him. I told him that I only pray in the name of Jesus, but that did not matter: "Pray for me, I know that God is with you." Students of years ago tell me that though they have forgotten my lectures, they do remember my prayers.

Still, when it comes down to brass tacks, my prayers do not seem to make much difference to people I pray for. When I pray that God will heal people with a terminal illness, they nevertheless die. Now and then, I pray that God will let someone die. A dear friend was unconscious and for several days had been breathing what was supposed to be his last breath, but he kept holding on to life. His family was spent, exhausted by days of hopeless waiting. I came into the room, kissed the man on the cheek, asked God to please take him. He died before I finished my prayer. But when I pray for people with inoperable cancer, they always die.

When I pray for people who are given a fighting chance, some of them get better, most of them die. And if they do get better, I have no way of knowing whether they would have gotten better had nobody prayed for them. Still, I keep on praying; if you meet me in a parking lot and stop to tell me your troubles, chances are that I will put my arm around you and pray that God will take your troubles away. Mostly, though, my prayers balance out between thanks for what I have and pleading for God to give poor people more to have and be thankful for. ✢

CHAPTER FIVE

Reprobate

As I slipped into my teens, I tested God's mercy by taking up a habit that the *Boy Scout Manual* called self-abuse, though the kids in my neighborhood had more user-friendly words for it. I was a single-sin sinner; I committed my share of others as well, I suppose, but I felt so guilty about this one that I had no mind for the others. I knew for sure that my sin was the worst of them all and that if God ever showed up and caught me in the act, he would, if he did not damn my soul, cause my right hand to wither limp like an empty glove dangling lifelessly from my wrist, the whole thing a fitting emblem of my sin and shame. What made things worse was that even though I felt worthy of God's wrath, I knew in my heart that I would revert to my secret pleasure, maybe the very next day.

At fifteen I had grown to an inch or two above six feet and weighed in at about ninety-five pounds, to anyone who saw me undressed a sure case of rickets. Later on, my mother accounted for my condition by saying that, exhausted as she was, she had had nothing to give me when I tried to feed from her breast. But her willingness to take the blame for my condition did not relieve me, and I struggled into puberty convinced that in God's eyes I was a disgusting sight and addicted to an evil habit to boot.

Actually, we did not talk very much about God at our house. We did not learn a catechism and we did not know any creed. But we did talk about our dominie, and about important people in general. We wondered, for instance, whether our dominie ever passed gas or did number two; my mother was sure he would not — could not — ever do such things. And we wondered whether the election of Franklin D. Roosevelt in 1932 was a signal that things had gotten so far out of hand that Jesus was likely to show up very soon to finish off our wicked world. The closest thing we had to instruction in the Christian religion was my mother's earnest plea that we never forget to pray, which may have had a more godly effect on us than any catechism.

My first encounter with real theology came one Sunday after the evening service when I listened in on a conversation the dominie was having with an elder on the stoop of the church. The elder asked the dominie what the doctrines of divine election and reprobation were all about and what the dominie said to the elder helped explain to me why I was the sinner that I was.

An eternity before a single human being stood on two legs, said the dominie, God could see in his imagination every man, woman, or child who was ever to be born of a woman. And he could also see that, once the first pair had fallen into sin, every last one of us would be born as a sinner worthy of damnation. Not wanting to see every last person on earth end up in hell, however, he selected a minority of them, but still an impressive number, to be saved. What about the others, the elder asked, those who did not get chosen? Ah, said the dominie, they are the reprobate, the poor souls whom God left out and targeted for damnation.

On hearing this, I knew for sure that I was one of the reprobate, chosen by God for damnation before I had ever taken a breath and leaving me without a chance. I was thrilled. Being personally selected by God, even if it be for damnation, gave me a certain distinction. Nobody singled out by God himself for perdition can be a nobody. And, besides, since I was targeted for hell anyway, I had nothing to lose. I could enjoy my sin while I had a chance to commit it.

I decided to begin my life of freedom with a new sin that was worse even then taking such guilty pleasure in abusing myself. What sin could possibly be worse? Maybe taking God's name in vain would do. I had never done any honest-to-goodness cussing and felt strange even thinking about it. But I would try. I considered whether I should cuss out loud or only in my head and decided that speaking it out loud would be worse than just thinking it. But what should I say? "Damn" seemed like a serious cuss, but it lacked profundity. I decided to go for broke — the cuss of the cursed, a damn with "God" in front of it. I would not ask him to damn anybody in particular, since I did not want anyone else to suffer for my sin. So I just added the impersonal pronoun "it," which could be just about anything. I said it out in the open while walking down Amity Street, loudly enough to catch the attention of anybody within thirty feet of me.

The earth did not shake. Day did not turn into night. God did not turn me into a pillar of salt. It was as if he did not really give a rip about my sins, and why should he? If he had already damned me for eternity, why should God care about my crummy sins in the meantime? But I did not have what it took to become a major-league sinner. If I did have it, I would probably have taken up serious full-time cussing, but as well as I can remember, I have never used the "G" word since. ✦

CHAPTER SIX

God and I at Muskegon High

To be frank about it, at Muskegon High I was a lonely loser, something to be pitied. As far as I could tell, nobody who knew me had any hope for me, and I had no hope for myself. To have hope you need to believe that what you hope for is possible. I had no such belief. I had imagination; I saw myself sometimes as a South American dictator with medals on every inch of my jacket, telling rapt audiences at the Berean Church how we did things in "my" country. But when I was not dreaming, I was a floating, dismal patch of fog.

Mrs. Sheridan, my tenth-grade English teacher, thought differently; she had hope for me. On the first day of class, wanting, I suppose, to know what sorts of kids she was going to have on her hands that semester, she asked us to write an autobiography in three pages. I wrote mine and handed it to her the next day. Two days later, after she had read them all, she stood near the door as we were leaving the class, took my arm, drew me a little closer, and said, "Lewis, you write well."

Mrs. Sheridan's words excited me into a frenzy of hope. In fact, they inspired me to think that being a journalist might just suit me when I grew up. I announced my future vocation at the supper table: "I think that I will be a journalist." I may as well have announced my intention to be a Nobel Laureate. "Oh, Lewis," they all chimed, "be practical for a change, don't have such big-shot ideas." I lost my faith again, and hope went down the drain with it.

Anyway, hope needs something else besides faith, and what it needs is desire. Passion maybe, the way Kierkegaard saw it — *passion for the possible.* To have hope you need to want something with all your heart. I did, now and then — when I dared — want to succeed in my studies. What I did not want was to try to succeed and then fail. I would rather be known as a boy who might have succeeded had he tried than as a poor sucker who tried and failed.

Oddly enough, however, I was as afraid of succeeding as I was of failing. The reason that success scared me was this: if I achieved at school, I would be expected to associate with other achievers, and the thought of an inferior person like me hobnobbing with successful students scared me away from making the effort.

Successful boys came from successful parents; their dads were doctors, or lawyers, or shopkeepers, or something else equally classy. And they were well off, the sort of people whose floors my mother scrubbed and whose underwear she washed. Their families went on vacations, their mothers played tennis, and they had parties on their birthdays. The achievers joined the clubs, acted in school plays, ran the student newspaper, got elected as class officers, and took it for granted that they would go to college, where they would succeed just as they did in high school. Not the kind of boys, in other words, who would want to be my friends. And certainly not the kind of girls who would waste a flirtation on me. Life inside the winners' circle looked to me like a fast fall into misery.

But I was not consistent. I did dream of doing better things, and maybe my dreams were revealing my real desires, or even my real hope, even, perhaps, my real self. For instance, why did I memorize Shakespeare's sonnets that no teacher had assigned me to read? One of the sonnets I memorized, Sonnet 29, came so close to my own feelings that I repeated it to myself so often that were I to live until I am a hundred and with a memory so debased that I cannot remember my middle name, I could still recite the whole of it at the drop of a hat. The first half of it is enough to show why I was so taken with it:

When, in disgrace with fortune and men's eyes,
I all alone beweep my outcast state,
And trouble deaf heaven with my bootless cries,
And look upon myself, and curse my fate,
Wishing me like to one more rich in hope,
Featured like him, like him with friends possessed,

Desiring this man's art and that man's scope,
With what I most enjoy contented least. . . .

There was Dostoyevski, too. I read him without any understanding, and yet with a sense that his darkest characters
had souls like mine. I also took up the tuba, the foot washer
to all other instruments, just so that I could join the school
band and play some good music. I played badly, but why, I
wonder, did I flirt with the very things I dared not embrace
in a classroom?

At church we had a young people's society where born-
again high school boys went to sing gospel choruses and
give their testimonies and meet Christian girls, though not
in that order. I was as afraid of this group as I was of the
successful kids at school, so I would arrive late on purpose
to avoid having to stand near the girls and jaw with the
boys. Sometimes, when I did arrive, I would draw the door
open a crack, look at all those happy kids' faces, lose my
nerve, tiptoe out of church, and walk around town long
enough to lead my mother to suppose that I had been in
good Christian company for the night.

About this same time, I lost my heart to a lovely Christian girl named Viola. Just looking at her inspired me to get
right with God so that I could get right with her. I set myself
to reading the Bible, especially St. Paul's letter to the
Romans and especially the first chapter, which raised the
possibility that I was one of those terrible people whom God

had abandoned to a swarm of ugly sins on grounds of their ingratitude for his blessings. But love drove me through my fears to the elders of the church, and I told them that I loved the Lord and wanted to live for him. Then I wept. I was welcomed into the fellowship, and was invited to take the sacrament of communion the very next week.

But I botched it. At our church, the communion bread was cut into bite-size squares and passed around on silver plates. The wine was passed in big goblets from which each communicant took a sip. I worried that I might drop the goblet and spill the holy wine on my Sunday suit. So I did not bring the cup of Christ's blood close enough to my lips to get a swallow. I took this to be an omen: God must have known that I might have drunk the cup unworthily and stepped in at the right moment to prevent me from drinking it to my own judgment.

In my family, work was a virtue standing head to head with prayer, so I found work as soon as I was old enough to dream that someone would hire me. As my first effort, I hung around a loading dock along with other unemployed men waited for a foreman to put them to work lugging boxes into a boxcar. I was looking for work, but when the foreman noticed that I had been hanging about a while, he told me to go play somewhere else. There were celery farms near our house, and I got my very first job planting baby celery plants that would grow in the greenhouse until they were sturdy enough to plant outside. I planted more weeds along with the celery than were acceptable and so the celery farmer did not ask me to come back.

I then thought up a devious way of finding a job. First I spent one night substituting for the dishwasher at a downtown restaurant. After that, I applied at the Walgreen Drug Store for a job at their lunch counter. "Any experience?" they asked. Yes, I said, I used to work at Sam's coffee shop. You're hired, the man said. I showed up for work the next Saturday, and they ushered me to a lunch counter two miles long, where I spent the day bringing people chicken salad after they had ordered the blue-plate special. At the end of the day the boss told me that he would call me when he wanted me to come back, which was never. On Monday I went to the Occidental Candy Shop, the sandwich and ice cream shop of choice for Muskegon's better-class people, where they came for hot-fudge sundaes after the show at the Michigan Theatre, which was the movie house of choice for the upper class. I told the proprietor that I had had experience at the Walgreen Drug Store. I was hired, and what did it matter if I had been hired at Walgreen's not to make hot-fudge Sundays, but to take orders for blue-plate specials?

Compared with high school kids today, I was a pretty innocent kid. I didn't do really bad things; I just didn't do many good things. I used no drugs. Smoked only a few cigarettes. Drank no booze. And never got close enough to a girl to be tempted to get closer. Mine were lonely sins. And if

God was walking with me through the halls of Muskegon Senior High, he seldom, if ever, let me know that he was there. ❖

CHAPTER SEVEN

God and I at Smedes Steel

About the time that I left high school, Neville Chamber-
lain, having made his last concession to Adolf Hitler,
arrived in London from Munich, stepped out of his air-
plane, black umbrella clutched under his right arm pit, and
announced that he had achieved "peace in our time." By the
end of that summer, Hitler had invaded Poland, and by late
fall, all of Europe was at war. I hardly noticed.

We were not a family to talk global politics, and, besides,
as the end of high school drew near, I had nothing in my
head but misty apprehensions about my own future. All I
had to show for myself was an academic record slanted toward failure, with no training or skill that might lead to a
trade and with a body that looked like a clothed clothes pole.
I had nothing in my pocket or in my head to recommend
me even to the cheapest or the least discriminating of colleges. My options were, to say the least, limited.

My Uncle Nick was my only hope. Uncle Nick was my
father's younger brother who had smuggled himself and

his wife and sister, my Aunt Jessie, illegally, over the Detroit river from Canada into the United States. They settled in Detroit, where he managed to pick up work at the Ford Motor Co. But he was no man to be tied to an assembly line, and he walked off the job before he drew his first paycheck.

Somewhere, he scavenged an abandoned forge, and, just as the Depression began to close down shops everywhere else, he opened up a blacksmith shop in his garage and nailed up a sign that announced: Smedes Iron Works. A decade later, as the threat of war had begun to nudge Detroit back to work, he moved out of his garage into a cement-block building with a lot beside it large enough to accommodate long steel beams, and he painted a sign on it that now read Smedes Steel. From here he began to provide builders everything in structural steel they needed to build tract houses for families who were moving into Detroit, where the jobs were.

I wrote to Uncle Nick and begged him for a job, admitting that my hands had never been of much use to anyone but promising that I would do my level best with what I had. Sure, he said, come on over. You can board with your Aunt Jessie for seven dollars a week out of the fourteen that you will be paid. Two Mondays later, I could be seen carrying a lunch box packed with three baloney sandwiches and walking to work at 7:30 AM in steel-toed shoes and blue work pants, a pale tower of flesh six foot three inches tall, now weighing in at 110 pounds, certainly a sorry-looking excuse for a steel worker.

I had enough talent, however, to grab an angle iron by a hook in each hand, dip it into a trough of black tar thinned out with gasoline, and stack it up on a pile to drip and to dry. After two hours of coating the angle irons, I would become drunk from the fumes and stagger out to the yard, where I sat on a beam for a few minutes to sober up. I painted steel beams out in the yard with the same gas and tar mixture but using a bucket and a brush, slapping the tar on all surfaces after the real steel men had cut the beams to size with acetylene torches. By the end of a year, I too had learned to cut beams to size and to weld plates to the ends of stanchions skillfully enough to make Uncle Nick think I might make a steel man after all.

After one year at it, however, I knew that God had not shaped me for steel, and I looked for ways to fill my life with something else. I had read in the *Detroit News* about night school courses that were offered free at Cass Tech High School in the heart of downtown Detroit. So on opening night I rode the Mack Avenue street car for about an hour and enrolled in two courses: typing, just in case I ever got to school, and radio drama, just to take my mind off of steel for two nights a week. Before the term was over, I had become the star of the radio drama class. One of the students was a leader in the United Auto Workers of America, and he told me that I could, if I had a feeling for the cause, have a fine future as a speaker for the union. I did not take the bait, but I did remember the offer and the memory murmured: "See? You really could be somebody if you wanted to be."

Meantime, loneliness was getting the better of me, as was my testosterone, two conditions to which even the shy and skinny are subject. Driven by these two spiritual needs, I would, on Saturdays, when we had half a day off, scrub the tar off my body, and then, about four in the afternoon, catch a street car and head off for the fleshpots that I had discovered in downtown Detroit. I would do a little shopping at Sam's Cut Rate, drink a beer, and eat a hamburger sandwich at one of the scruffy cafés tucked into slots off the better streets. Then, by which time it had gotten dark, I would walk over to the Uptown Burlesque and settle into a balcony seat to take in a forbidden show. Stars like Rose La Rose and Ruby La Rue brought my testosterone to a wicked boil. They swirled their hips and bumped their buttocks to the hard beat of a bass drummer, and, before my very eyes, dropped almost every thread of their flimsy clothing, piece by naughty piece, until, when only their most private parts were still covered, they wrapped the stage curtain around their nearly naked bodies and gave us one last wink before they disappeared.

How could a Christian young man of eighteen expect to get right with God while he was despising the honest work that God, in his goodness, had provided him; while he was wasting his strength at night school on such unmanly things as typing and radio drama; and while, to top it off, he was awakening unthinkable lusts by watching wicked women take their clothes off on Saturday evenings — this sorry spectacle to be followed then, on the Lord's Day morning, by sitting in the pew at Aunt Jessie's church and inventing techniques for tucking my chin between my fingers so that I could sleep through the sermon without my head bobbing for everybody to see?

On the other hand, as a pious contradiction, when night fell on Sunday, I attended revival meetings that I had tracked in the Saturday edition of the *Detroit News*. Big-time show-biz evangelists like Bob Jones and Gypsy Smith seemed to speak more directly to my soul than did the sedate preacher at Aunt Jessie's church. Sometimes, for an hour or so, I felt as if I were being enveloped in saving grace, but by the time I got off the street car I was again sinking into a double dose of guilt.

Since I had discovered that steel was not my vocation, I began to look for a place to get some education. I knew that I was not rich enough — and I suspected that I was not smart enough — for college, so I began to focus on the Moody Bible Institute in Chicago, where tuition was free and academic intelligence was nowhere near a priority. Uncle Nick and Aunt Jessie told me that I was a fool to leave a good job where, if I just put my heart into it, I could soon be making as much as twenty dollars a week and go cruising around with Christian girls in my own Model A Ford. Besides, they wondered, what could put it into my head to go to Moody Bible when I did not even like going to church?

About this time, something happened to me at the docks where freighters brought steel beams and stanchions to Detroit from further east on Lake Erie. The Teamsters Union had called a strike and no steel was being trucked from the docks to Detroit's providers. We at Smedes Steel ignored the strike and drove a couple of trucks down to the docks, loaded our steel beams, and hauled them back to the shop.

Gigantic cranes hoisted the steel beams from boat to dock by means of immense electro-magnets, each of them about three feet thick, eight feet in diameter, and weighing about fifteen tons. The magnets hung at the end of a two-inch cable which was, in turn, controlled by an operator sitting in a cab above the docks. I was standing on the ground blankly watching the theater of steel bustling around me when a shadow fell over me, which seemed odd because there were no trees or building that could cast a shadow.

I looked up and saw one of the immense magnets ten feet above me. Stevedores ducked in and under these magnets all day long without giving them a thought, but I did not feel safe with that monster hovering over me, so I took a long step away. At that instant, the magnet crashed to earth and scraped the heel of my shoe as it landed. Rushing to investigate, the crane operator discovered that the cable holding the tons of magnetized steel above my head had been frayed down to a few threads of wire just before it crashed.

Later on, away from the docks, I wondered whether God himself could have pushed me out of the way of that magnet just in time to save my neck and get my attention at the same time. It seemed absurd to wonder whether the Maker of the Universe would go to such extreme lengths to get the attention of a failed steel man. But then again, I had been less than a tenth of a second away from being crushed to the thickness of a dime, and such things do not happen every day. Maybe God was trying to tell me that he approved of my plan to find him at Moody and maybe even find a future for myself. Whether or not God was giving me the high sign, I kissed Smedes Steel good-by and headed off for Moody Bible. ✢

CHAPTER EIGHT

God and I at Moody Bible

I chucked my tar-stiffened pants, my tar-coated shoes, and my tar-smeared shirts into a garbage can, packed my bag, said good-by to Aunt Jessie, hitchhiked back to Muskegon, and stunned my family by announcing that I had left Uncle Nick's steel shop and was going to Chicago to enroll at the Moody Bible Institute. I packed my stuff in a beat-up suitcase that I had bought at a pawn shop, and I walked downtown to the bus depot, got on a Greyhound bus, and headed for Chicago. My mother walked to the depot with me, which moved my spirit considerably, and I saw from the window of the bus that she was weeping as she waved good-by.

Once I had become a registered Moody student and after I had learned the rules, I endeavored to get myself in synch with Moody's life-style. We were there not by right but by privilege, we were told, and the only sure way to stay there was to obey the rules: no dating during the first semester, only suit coats and ties in the classroom as well as at every meal, weekly reports of how much time we spent at prayer, how many gospel tracts we had given away, and how many souls we had saved.

I followed the rules, but I never did master the Moody accent. I could not get myself to say "Praise the Lord" as if it were a punctuation mark. Or that "I was led of the Lord" as my reason for doing whatever it was that I happened to be doing. For a little while I signed my letters off with "Yours in Christ," but it seemed like something I would not do of my own accord, and I soon switched back to "Yours truly."

The reputation that most students prized was that they had a "passion for souls" and were "on fire for the Lord." I did not develop a "passion for souls" and had not caught on fire, and my failure disturbed me considerably. How could I not have a passion for souls when people walking down the street at that very moment might perish forever in hell because I failed to witness to them about Jesus? Their damnation would be on my head forever. Alone in my dormitory room at night, I would ask myself: why sit I here idle when I could be out on the street witnessing to sinners who might die and go to hell if I do not give them another chance to accept Christ? So, gospel tracts in hand, I hustled over to the lovely park in front of the famous Newbury Library, a square block that had become Chicago's version of London's Hyde Park and came to be known locally as Bug-house Square. Once there, I would sidle up to people who were listening to one of the soapbox orators and offer them a gospel tract.

I was often suckered into arguments over diversionary issues like whether Christians were any better than other people.

"You mean to tell me that if some gorgeous broad showed up right now and invited you up to her apartment, you would not go?"

"No, sir," I said, knowing that if someone so described invited me anywhere at all, I would be too scared to go.

"I don't believe you, kid, you guys are no better than the rest of us, so buzz off."

Which I did.

A passion for souls? Any souls in particular? No, just souls in general. I couldn't help it; I didn't have that passion.

I have, over the years, developed a passion for people, not people in general, but persons in particular, and not just for their souls. I have an honest-to-goodness passion for certain children in Los Angeles, innocent as newborn kittens, knocked around, forgotten, abandoned by their parents, and plunked into the Los Angeles Child Welfare Department, which may not be the ultimate, but still a very real, hell. I have a passion for people of my age, without memory, without hope, stuck like living corpses in dysfunctional nursing homes. I have a passion for persons I know who need to be saved from their sins so that they can go to heaven, but for now need to be saved from AIDS and saved from hunger and saved from hopelessness.

I did all right at my studies, and that pleased me until I had the sense to notice that one would have to be a borderline dolt to fail at them. At Moody Bible we were not encouraged to study the Bible with any real seriousness. There were exceptions; every now and then a new teacher would shock us all by expecting some mental effort from us. For the most part, however, independent thinking was discouraged as if it were the eighth cardinal sin.

Certain Moody people noticed that when I read the Bible aloud I accented the right phrases, and others noticed that when I wrote something it came out in proper sentences. As a result, I was tagged for two plum student jobs. First I was hired as a radio announcer at WMBI, "The Radio Voice of the Moody Bible Institute." Then I was appointed to be the editor of *The Moody Student,* a weekly that looked for all the world like any other student paper, but was actually an organ of the public relations department. My job was to publish the sort of thing that would assure the donors that all was well at the school that D. L. Moody founded.

But I had a few naughty ideas for pumping a little life into the paper. I would, for instance, write a mild editorial one week and then, the next week, I would write and publish a blistering letter opposing it. I was summoned to the PR office and was told that even if it was not my fault that people sent me nasty letters, I was not expected to print them.

My life as broadcaster and editor ended suddenly one

morning when I found a notice in my mail box that sum-moned me to the office of the superintendent of male stu-dents. The facts were that I had received another student's package by mistake and had made a much bigger mistake of my own by taking the elevator up one floor of the women's dormitory to deliver it to its rightful recipient. My errand done, the elevator operator, a female student, called the superintendent of women as soon as I was out of sight. That was Sunday morning. Monday morning I was relieved of both of my nifty jobs.

I had come to Moody with a sincere hope of coming to terms with God. I was making very little progress, however, and my main handicap was that I could not fit Moody's por-trait of a person who was saved from future hellfire and was now on fire for the Lord. The Moody model became to me what the law of God had become to St. Paul: I had no argu-ment with the model, it was just that I couldn't live up to it. And not living up to it, I was *at* Moody but not *of* Moody, and maybe not of God either. God was gone again.

But he met me again at a used book store. I was brows-ing there, picked up a thin volume called *The Rest of Faith*, and read it in the aisle between the stacks. The author, who-ever he was, told me that if I wanted to come to terms with God, it had to be on his terms, the chief one being that I would have to give up my ridiculous notion that I would be accepted by God only if I had what it took to be a very proper Moody type. What I needed to do was to let him accept me with no consideration of whether I was either acceptable or unacceptable. And then, when I had done that, to quit stewing about it and just rest in the fact that I was loved and accepted by God, no strings attached. Odd that it should have taken me so long to get the point. ✝

CHAPTER NINE

God and I at Calvin College

While I was still groping for God at Moody Bible, the Japanese bombed Pearl Harbor and America entered the war. I signed up and went to have my physical. But when I took off my clothes, the sergeant took a quick look at my naked body, winced, suppressed giggles, and told me to go home and come back when I had gotten a little *meat* on my bones. I went to a Red Cross station to give my blood, the very least I could do for my country, but they told me that I needed every drop that I had. So having been snatched from sudden death at the steel docks, saved by grace in a secondhand book store, rejected by the military, and now released by Moody Bible, I had a hunch that the constellation of these events might be a sign that I was meant to go to college and maybe even become a preacher of some sort. Besides which, with the army and navy grabbing every healthy male they could get their hands on, even good colleges were accepting any male applicant who had a high school diploma in his hands and some tuition money in his pocket.

I was accepted by Calvin College, a serious liberal arts school in Grand Rapids, Michigan, that was owned and operated by Dutch Calvinists who wanted their children to get the intellectual equipment they needed to serve God and bring a patch of his Kingdom into his broken world. Getting an education for the sake of becoming an educated man or woman never entered their heads. Nor did they calculate the college graduate's chances for a better income. The only reason for higher education was service in the Kingdom of God.

The first class of the first day of my first semester was English composition. The teacher was Jacob Vandenbosch, getting along in years at the time, with a gleaming bald head that arose like a bare butte atop his shoulders, his voice nasal and thin, and wearing a practiced grin that conveyed a worn patience more than it did a happiness of spirit.

Jacob Vandenbosch introduced me that day to a God the likes of whom I had never even heard about — a God who liked elegant sentences and was offended by dangling modifiers. Once you believe this, where can you stop? If the Maker of the Universe admired words well put together, think of how he must love sound thought well put together; and if he loved sound thinking, how he must love a Bach concerto; and if he loved a Bach concerto, think of how he prized any human effort to bring a foretaste, be it ever so small, of his Kingdom of justice and peace and happiness to the victimized people of the world. In short, I met the

Maker of the Universe, who loved the world he made and was dedicated to its redemption. I found the joy of the Lord, not at prayer meeting, but in English Composition 101.

Later on I would hear a theologian say that sinners needed two conversions, first a conversion from the world to Christ and second a conversion from Christ back to the world. Calvin College was where I had the second conversion. I began to see a vision of Christ not as the world's enemy, but as its best friend. Not as one whose coming would spell the end of human civilization but as one who, when he came, would heal all of its grave diseases and make it over into his Kingdom of peace and justice — do it so thoroughly that it could be called a new creation.

Early on at college, it occurred to me that I may also have been wrong about my intellectual deficiency. When I received my grades for my first semester's work, I was stunned to discover that I had received a 4.00 grade point average, as high as it can get. At first I figured that this was just a fluke; my grades for the second semester would bring me down to earth with a thud. But the miracle repeated itself. I was after all a person with intellectual promise. And with the birth of my new sense of who I was and what I could do, I began a new leg on my journey with God.

One of the best gifts that God gave me at college was some good friends. The dearest of them all was, of all things, a student by the name of Calvin, Calvin Bulthuis. Another was Dirk Jellema, a son of William Harry Jellema, the father figure to a distinguished line of philosophers who would teach at Calvin and elsewhere. There were other friends, splendid all of them, but Cal and Dirk became my closest friends and stayed close until each of them died.

My college friends not only made my life more interesting than it had ever been, they made it easier for me to settle into my new faith. Cal and Dirk did not talk all that much about their faith, but they talked constantly about how to practice it. They did not put their souls on the table for the three of us to examine. They did not talk all that much about Jesus either, but when they did talk about him, they brought me to attention. I remember a beer-moistened conversation during which Dirk remarked that whenever he thought about the incarnation of the Son of God, chills ran up and down his back. (As for the beer, Dirk liked to quote G. K. Chesterton as saying that beer and Bible were the two best B's in the English language.)

They seemed to accept their faith as the pivot of their own identity. They took God himself for granted as the core of the universe. In fact, their seriousness about God gave them a sense of humor about some of the church's sacred traditions. Together with a few other friends, we wrote and published a small book called *Youth Speaks on Calvinism*. It became a *cause celebre* of sorts in the world of Dutch Calvinism. We did not level a single complaint about the doctrines of Calvinism, but we did recommend some new strategies for practicing it. Our humorless church fathers, however, took it as a minor revolution against the tradition and a major assault on them personally.

We had some truly great teachers, some quaintly mediocre teachers, and some true duds at Calvin. But all of them owned the Calvinist's "world and life view." Faith in Christ not only gave us hope for life in heaven, it gave us a point of view for valuing life on earth. That view can be summed up in four short sentences.

1. In the beginning, God made the world wonderfully good.
2. Near the start, the human family brought evil into the world's awesome goodness.
3. In the end, God will come to fix his world and make it altogether good again.
4. In between, his children are to go into the world and create some imperfect models of the good world to come.

This is the Calvinism to which I was converted in college. It is the faith that has sustained my spirit ever since. I cherish it because it carries a magnificent hope inside of it. Though it brings grief that the world is as badly broken as it is, it offers hope that there is still enough goodness in the world to make it both fixable and worth fixing. ✦

CHAPTER TEN

Becoming Christian Reformed

At Calvin College I had found my place among my kind of people. It was a Christian community that loved God's world no less for loving his Word, and was dedicated to bringing that world, at least in snippets, here and there, a mite closer to what its Maker had in mind when he made it. It was also a community that felt free to taste, enjoy, and take nourishment from all the good gifts of the human spirit from whatever spirit it comes. So, intellectually and spiritually I was, for the first time in my life, at peace with God and at home with his people.

I was, however, a member of no church. I had grown up in the Berean Church of Muskegon, Michigan, which specialized in biblical prophecies about the end of the world in general and about what God has in mind for the Jews in particular. (The pastor, a man of impressive intellect and piety, had been defrocked by the Christian Reformed Church because of his peculiar way of sizing up what the Bible had to say about how things are going to turn out in the end.) At that time, however, prophecies about the end of the world did not much speak to my condition, and the church closest at hand to me now was the church that my idolized professors called theirs. Any church where superb Christians like these were at home was, I figured, more than good enough for me. So I made my confession and was received into the church as a bona fide communicant.

It was not as though I had scouted out all the other churches that dotted the American landscape and had by processes of elimination come to the conclusion that this church, the Christian Reformed Church, was the purest and best of them all. Nor did I join the Christian Reformed Church because I believed that every sentence of its dogmas was true; more than likely I came to believe its dogmas because I joined the church. Nor did I join this church with a mission to improve it; I was a seeker, not a crusader, and, besides, the church struck me as being just fine the way it was.

What, then, led me to join? I joined this small church because it had a great vision of God as the Creator and the Redeemer of the whole wide world. I also liked its orderliness, its sobriety, and its respect for education. I liked the practice of baptizing babies into the family of God and bringing them up as children of God and not as lost sinners who still had to walk down the sawdust trail to get saved. I also liked its modest expectations of our spiritual improvement. The Heidelberg Catechism, everyone's favorite creed, taught that we can expect no more from ourselves in this life than a small beginning into holiness and wholeness. And this comforted me in view of the sluggish pace of my own spiritual improvement. But, when I get right down to it, I joined the Christian Reformed Church mostly because it was the church of the teachers whom I had so much admired at Calvin.

I soon learned, however, that these large-spirited people connected with the college were not typical of Christian Reformed people as a whole. Christian Reformed folks were, like me, children of immigrants, some of them immigrants themselves, and most of them felt like strangers in a foreign land. The more conservative leaders among them tended to see the American world as the whore of Babylon hell-bent on seducing their children from the Dutch Reformed way of faith and life. They especially feared the pleasures that American society tempted them with, the most dangerous of which were the theater, games of chance, and dancing. But they were just as leery of the American churches — the liberal ones of course, but the evangelical ones too, what with their mushy indifference to muscular Reformed doctrine. The only safe strategy was isolation.

Joining the church was something like getting married: neither of us had a notion of what we were getting into. It had no idea of what it had on its hands with me. I had no idea how long it would take before an adopted child into this ethnic-immigrant-dogmatic family could feel that he truly was a member of the family. I was now and then reminded by one of my Calvin professors that I was an "outsider" and should ask for no special favors. Adopting me as one born out of ecclesiastical wedlock, the church fathers were not convinced that I had been purged of the virus of my past associations.

The guardians of our Zion were right to worry about me. Locking the mysteries of my faith within precise dogmatic definitions did not suit me well. I needed some intellectual room in my faith to wiggle, to explore, to wonder, to doubt, and to make mistakes. I liked such phrases as "on the other hand" or "and yet" or "let's have another look." Such language made the conservative clergy nervous.

The deepest difference between my professors and the conservative clergy was about how Christian believers should relate to the world of unbelievers. The conservative ministers believed that believers and unbelievers were separated by a chasm so deep and so wide that no bridge could be built across it for people on both sides to cross over and learn from each other. The only safe way to keep people from falling into the chasm was to erect invisible walls at its edge. Others, like my professors, believed that believers and unbelievers had enough in common to build bridges to cross over the gap to meet each other. Call one group Christians of the wall or Christians of the gap; they dedicated themselves to sealing the borders to keep the strangers from coming over. Call the other group Christians of the bridge; they did not ignore the reality of the gap, but they wanted to build bridges for people on both sides of it to cross over and learn from each other.

I was, from the start, a Christian of the bridge. I liked bridges that I could cross over to drink from unbelievers' goblets, to feast on their wisdom, and to admire their good works. I also liked bridges that I could cross over and, with God's blessing, be a blessing to the people on the other side.

What I lacked most, in the eyes of gap people, however, was what snobs today call *gravitas,* or graveness; I seemed to lack the serious sobriety fitting for a vigorous defender of the Reformed faith. I did not espouse heresies, but neither was I theologically armed and ready to shoot it out over them either. Sometimes even the metaphors I used to express the faith disturbed them. Metaphors, they thought, were for frivolous poetry, not for matters as serious as the Reformed truth. Using metaphors came too close to what the Dutch called *spotten,* which meant to make light of serious things.

One short story, from later in my life, will illustrate.

In the early seventies Henry Stob, one of my college heroes, wanted me to succeed him as the Professor of Christian Ethics at Calvin Theological Seminary. In those days, only the General Synod of the church could decide who was and who was not qualified to teach its future ministers. A vote had to be taken. I was one of three candidates. But certain delegates to the Synod had disturbing concerns about me. I had once admitted that I harbored a hope that everybody would go to heaven, a hope that made me suspect for having it. They asked the Synod to summon me from California to Grand Rapids for a cross-examination. Which it did.

I took a United flight out of Los Angeles the next day on a Boeing 707, the plane with a long, narrow cabin shaped like a panatela cigar that could be a torture to passengers like myself who were afflicted with claustrophobia. I needed to switch planes in Chicago and the weather there was bad. So, not being able to land, our plane was stacked up with many other planes in a blinking spiral above O'Hare airport. We circled for as long as our fuel held out. Before it gave out entirely, the pilot flew us back to Des Moines, Iowa, and refueled. Again, we took our place over Chicago, and again, we ran low on fuel. This time we flew to St. Louis for a new tankful. Almost all of us were strangers to each other. Supplies of food and drink were gone. The flight lasted eighteen hours.

The next day I stood in the dock before the Synod. The first person to challenge my orthodoxy went straight for the jugular: What did I think of hell? I replied that, on that particular day, I thought of hell as being seat-belted in a fully packed 707 flying with a crowd of strangers over O'Hare airport for all eternity. To a serious Synod, deliberating on the Lord's business, what I said sounded like insufferable levity, and they responded with blue-blooded Calvinistic *gravitas.* Still, in spite of my unacceptable jocularity, I think that I received at least 20 votes from the 200 delegates.

My church is no longer the same church that it was when I joined it. I would not say that the change has been totally for the better, but I am sure that it was inevitable. With the eventual departure of its most able and combative conservative leaders, the church has lost the people whose sport was heresy hunting and whose stock-in-trade was wall building. My guess is that the sport of heresy hunting lost its lure one bad day when the General Synod of the church rebuked a professor for daring — at Christmastime, mind you — to write that God loved all the children of the world. That, I guess, was the day when we lost our taste for dogmatic precision and when few of us remained fans of theological donnybrooks. Meanwhile, whatever it was about me that sometimes stretched the patience of the fathers, I am grateful that Doris and I have walked with God in the church's embrace. ❖

CHAPTER ELEVEN

Looking for God
at Theological Seminary

I graduated from Calvin College in 1946. My next step to-wards the ministry would be to move into a theological seminary. I was expected to walk toward the edge of the college campus and enroll at Calvin Seminary. But I had heard that interesting things were being said and done at Westminster Seminary in Philadelphia, and that is where I went.

The chief attraction there was a Dutch Calvinist by the name of Cornelius Van Til, who was what insiders called a "presuppositional" thinker. What this meant was that any thinking person's grasp of reality was set beforehand by the presuppositions which that person had accepted about God and reality. What we believe to be the source and sustainer of all reality determines how we see reality itself. Thus if anyone at all, philosopher or plumber, makes wrong assumptions (or has wrong beliefs) about ultimate reality, she fundamentally distorts everything she tries to understand about finite reality. Even though she is a John Nash at pure mathematics, she would miss genuine mathematical truth until she changed her assumptions about God. Even though Einstein formulated the theory of relativity, if he did not have the true faith, he had to have gotten relativity basically wrong.

I was mesmerized for one semester by the boldness of Van Til's thinking, but by the second semester I began to suspect that he was stretching a defensible theory of knowledge to the borders of absurdity. If true, it would mean that unless any two people had correct beliefs about God and about the world they could not have a genuine conversation about anything. How can two people talk respectfully together about interesting parts of reality — the economy, for instance, or the possibility of life on Mars — if one of them assumes that everything the other person says about anything is doomed to be dead wrong?

Van Til was convinced that if anyone's assumptions about God are wrong, she cannot be trusted even when she says that she believes the gospel truth about Jesus. He wrote a book called *The New Modernism* in which he contended that the star theologian of the century, Karl Barth, was a modernist because, in Van Til's view, he denied that Jesus was God in human form and denied as well that he had risen from the dead. The hitch was that Barth had affirmed these things over and over and, in fact, was largely to be credited with bringing the gospel back into the churches of Europe. But Van Til said that even if Barth shouted from the tower of St. Peter's that Jesus was the Son of God, he *could* not believe what he was saying. His philosophical presuppositions would not let him.

Several years later, after I had finished my graduate studies in Amsterdam, I had occasion to put the question to Barth himself: "Sir, if you will permit me an absurd anachronism, let us suppose that a journalist carried a camera into Jesus' tomb about eight o'clock on Easter Sunday morning and took pictures of every inch of the tomb, what would have showed up on his film?" Barth sighed. This again? He had been asked questions like this by every skeptical evangelical who got within shouting distance of him. But he was patient: "He would have gotten nothing but pictures of an empty tomb. Jesus was not there. He had walked out of the tomb early that morning."

I told Van Til about this conversation. His answer was, for me, a final exhibition of intellectual futility. "Smedes," he said, "you have studied philosophy, you should know that Barth *cannot* believe that Jesus rose from the dead." Cannot! Not merely does not, but *cannot* believe what he said he believed. Conversation finished.

I left Westminster after one year and went back to Grand Rapids and Calvin Seminary. At Calvin Seminary we learned the craft of being a minister. In those days we did not explore the truth; we memorized it. Our dogmas were never examined in the light of others; others were always judged in the light of ours. The teachers themselves suffered under heavy burdens of incompetence, and, to make matters worse, they were a contentious bunch; each of them carefully nursed petty grudges against at least one of his colleagues. My memory needs a booster shot of grace before it can recall a single seminary class that enriched my perception of God, deepened my commitment to Christ, or sent me home eager to explore these things further. Two years after I left seminary, all of its professors, except for one, were fired.

I did, however, do two things outside of the classroom during those two years that were to affect my future walk with God.

After my first year at Calvin Seminary, I was given a summer assignment to a rather large congregation in Sanborn, Iowa, which did not have a pastor at the time. Sanborn was a small town without an interesting or elegant thing in it. But the lushness of the fields of corn and grain around it more than made up for its own plainness. The people in my congregation were, for the most part, successful farmers, generous people, sturdy believers who came to church every bright Sunday morning and every sleepy afternoon to hear from a novice preacher the same sort of sermons that their fathers and mothers had heard in the same church.

I got along well with those farmers. I liked them. They liked me and thought I was a fair preacher; in fact, when I finished my education, theirs was one of the churches that called me to be their minister. One way they showed their affection during that summer was by leaving at our back door bottles of whipping cream, home-churned butter, free-ranging chickens, and a superb assortment of green vegetables. After ten weeks on this diet, I had metamorphosed from a six-foot three-inch boy of 120 pounds into an adequate man of 180 pounds.

I discovered there that I could preach sermons in a language that uneducated (though intelligent) farm folk found easy to grasp and, now and then, even interesting. And, to my lasting surprise, I discovered that those sermons and that language were genuinely mine.

The second thing I did during my Calvin Seminary days that affected my later studies was to write a contest paper on "Athanasius's Role in the Arian Controversy"; being the only student who entered the contest, I won. Athanasius was the fourth-century church father who persuaded the whole church that Jesus was truly God, through and through, and not, as some upstarts were saying, the creature closest of any to God but not God himself.

The often scandalous drama of this watershed controversy fascinated me, but Athanasius's reason for saying that Jesus had to be God seemed odd to me and it puzzled me. He had one argument to support his view and he hammered on it repeatedly: Jesus had to be God *in order to make us gods.*

Tell that to a Calvinist! Nothing we could say about ourselves could be more scandalous to a Calvinist than that we could get to be gods. I did not know it then, but I would soon be spending a lot of time poking around in this scandalous notion that we poor sinful creatures are ripe for deification. ✢

CHAPTER TWELVE

My Doris and I

I proposed to Doris Dekker by long-distance telephone the day after she got home from a Thanksgiving Day weekend she had spent with me in Philadelphia. We had had a splendid time together and I had meant to propose marriage to her before her train left. But I lost my nerve at the last minute and watched the train chug her back — unasked — to Grand Rapids. She — at her end of the telephone — had nerve enough for both of us; her answer came back to me like the very punctuation of my question.

Doris's father, Harry, was a chemistry professor at Calvin. Her mother, Mae, never went to college. Mae's mother believed that God made women significantly less than men and that sending daughters to college along with their brothers would only arouse in them an unbiblical lust for equality, which, in turn, would make them unfit to be subservient wives. But, deprived of higher education as she may have been, Mother Mae was ready to prove that she was the equal of any Ph.D. who might come along.

Tall, handsome, and stately in her walk, Mae would stride down the aisle to the Dekker pew on Sunday morning as if daring the preacher to say that *her* children were born totally depraved. When the mood was on her, she would sit at her piano in the living room and, from memory, accompany herself as she sang — in German — whatever of Schubert's *Lieder* came to her mind. She loved Goethe and would, at anybody's encouragement, recite — in German — line after line of his poetry. Shakespeare? Name the play or the sonnet that pleased you, and she would lift her chin an inch and over it would pour as many lines as you had time for.

Thanks to a mother like Mae, the Calvinist doctrine of total depravity never had a real chance with Doris. She saw no reason for disputing the depressing dogma as long as it did not interfere with her simple faith that, all things considered, she was, deep inside, a rather splendid creature. Living with Doris has led me to suspect that, knowing little and caring even less about the spiritual dynamics that made the human psyche tick, the Reformers used the doctrine as a link in the logic of saving grace: admit that you are totally depraved and you will never be seduced with the fantasy that we can play even a minor role in our salvation. Even though the dogma is enshrined in the creeds, it has not infected the healthier spirits among believers.

I mention this because Doris's positive feelings about herself have helped me in my battle with depressing feelings about myself. She was too smart to try to convince me that I was really a fine fellow; her method was to persuade me that if I had to be the kind of nut who gets a kick out of beating on his own soul, I should resign myself to my own wackiness and trust that God has grace for fools as well as for sinners. Her wisdom ultimately got through to me: I needed to accept myself as a neurotic who too often thinks that he is a hopeless human being. She also helped me by hinting that my bloated mea culpas were turning me into a tiresome bore.

Another thing about Doris is her zero tolerance of fakery. You will never hear her using it to describe herself, but the word for her is *authenticity*. She likes things that look like what they are. For instance, she hates plastic when it is disguised to look like something that is not plastic. These days you can lay a whole floor with plastic slats that look exactly like the real wood you get from a tree — maple, oak, walnut, or exotic teak; she is not impressed.

She feels the same way about evangelical jargon and evangelical posturing. She seems to have a gift of intuition that unerringly spots fake piety, whether it is put on by a showboat evangelist or a lugubrious bishop. And I have long ago learned that she can see it in me whenever I try to get by with it.

Authenticity, it seems to me, is a species of honesty, a way of being a truthful person, that refers to something more than usually telling the truth. The difference is that

Doris simply cannot tell a lie — cannot tell even white lies, not even tiny little innocent white lies that might make life a trifle more agreeable for someone than the brutal truth would. It is not as if she is a poor hand at lying; she is, like God, unable to lie.

Still, in a pinch, when she wants to be, at the same time, both caring and honest, she has her own way of avoiding cruel truth. If on any Christmas Eve one of our kids gives her a gift that challenges her taste, she just bends the truth a bit; it is *very interesting,* she may say, and since we have all caught on, we chalk it up as love. There have been occasions in which I have wished she were able to tell a tender white lie. But to wish her to lie is like wishing turtles to fly. It is, I grant you, a crude metaphor. The turtle is earthbound by its fate to wear a heavy shell; Doris is truth bound by her own choice. A turtle has bulk, she has character.

Her authenticity has protected her from the virus of evangelical hyperbole that has settled where we live in Southern California. Dependable old words don't work here in California anymore. Even the word "good" has gone bad on us; being "pretty good" is a minor disgrace. A critic can kill a movie's chances by calling it merely good. I know of a preacher who forbids staff members to say, if asked, that they are pretty good; for servants of God only fantastic is acceptable.

Living, as we have for almost thirty-five years, in the birthplace of hyperbole, Doris still means GOOD when she says "good." Her authenticity is, I believe, a trademark of godliness. I would not trade three minutes of her God-walk for ten hours of glib God-talk. And if eating breakfast every morning and going to bed every night with someone as authentic as Doris has not nurtured in my heart a yen to be a more honest man, I would indeed be as hopeless as I have sometimes thought I was. Living with her all this time, I have come to want nothing in the world more than the faith to be honest with God and the respect to be honest with his people. I am not as honest as she is — not by a long shot — but I do wish I were.

I must tell you just one more thing about Doris that has made God's odd ways more endurable for me. I am not sure whether I shall be talking about hope or courage. Both, I think, because courage is really a species of hope: we have courage to face danger only when we have hope of getting beyond it.

For strength, Doris drinks from hope. I am not talking here about the Christian hope of heaven. She takes heavenly hope in good faith, even though she evinces no fierce desire to get there soon. The hope I admire in Doris has the shape of courage to walk straight into trouble with eyes wide open right here on earth. No matter how miserable things get, she believes that they can get better, and because she has hope, she is willing to live with them until they do get better.

Unexpected adversity does not floor her, especially not

when she is the person most threatened by it. A couple of weeks after we had arrived in California, Doris learned that she had breast cancer and needed surgery right away. Her first thought was for the kids; being yanked from their home and school and friends in Michigan was more than enough to unsettle them, but if we added fear for their mom's life, we were likely to turn their anxiety into dread. So Doris made a plan; we would talk about the surgery as if it were almost an everyday thing, go to church Sunday morning, have a picnic afterward, and then deliver Mom to the City of Hope (which is a renowned research center and hospital for people with catastrophic disease).

As it turned out, however, someone in the church had learned about her cancer and asked the visiting preacher to mention Doris in his prayer. Which he did, with an overdose of well-meant pastoral empathy, going on and on about the tragedy that had befallen the Smedes family, and then getting to his sermon. He took as his text the prophet's word to King Hezekiah: THIS DAY THOU SHALT SURELY DIE. The sermon done, he instantly gave as an encore a mournful prayer for Mrs. Smedes. But if you had watched Doris herd the kids afterwards to the car, you would have thought that she had heard not a word.

A few years after her surgery Doris was offered a chance to have a surgeon cut out a few dispensable body muscles, shape them into the likeness of a breast, and fix the tissue to the flat side of her chest. This was early in the history of breast replacement and the plastic surgeons were looking for volunteers to practice on. No thanks, Doris said, if a one-breast woman is what I am, a one-breast woman I shall be. No fooling around with reality. If I had problems with her decision, she would trust me to deal with them.

That was a long time ago. These days, when we thank God for the affection and virtues of our grown-up adopted children, I sometimes look back in gratitude to darker days of fear and foreboding for their futures. Adopted children, no matter where they come from, enter a family with deeper problems than most adoptive parents realize. For adoptive parents to embrace someone else's child is the easy part. For adopted babies to be torn from the mother who gave them birth is the hard part. Babies are not puppies; they cannot be taken from their mothers without suffering a psychic trauma that goes deeper into their souls than most of us can guess.

Doris and I believed that what would of course be our uncommonly intelligent parenting would spare *our* adopted kids from such troubles. About the time our daughter, the oldest of the three, was getting to be a precocious adolescent, we learned how naïve we had been. The right title of her teenage story could only be *The Tempest*. Later on, she wrote about her search for her biological mother and, among other insightful observations, she said that her goal at our house was to prove that if she could make us miserable enough, we would abandon her too. Making her parents' life miserable was easy; getting them to abandon her was impossible.

In my hysteria, I knew for sure that she would end up on Sunset Boulevard homeless and addicted and that it would be my fault. Doris knew with the nervous courage of hope that Cathy's coming days would be better than those she had had. She kept her head and she kept her faith; if it was God who gave us this daughter, it would be God who would keep her off the evil ways. Doris's courage carried me along and even gave me a little courage of my own.

Doris's impact on my life with God has been subtle, indirect, and silent. She did not nag me or even pray me towards a deeper faith. But one reason that I have clung to my veiled God is that my transparent wife has clung to me. She has been her own contagiously healthy spirit, and my designated hoper. I will tell you this and then I will stop: walking with God has been for me inseparable from walking with Doris. ✢

CHAPTER THIRTEEN

God and I in Amsterdam

I n the spring of my last year at seminary, while my classmates were praying for a call from the congregation of their choice, I was making up my mind about where I should do graduate studies. Princeton Seminary offered some money, but Dutch universities charged no tuition at all. Besides, the Free University of Amsterdam had been the intellectual fountainhead of Dutch Calvinism, and I thought that since I was a convert and not a native son, I should go there to study the sources. I knew that I was getting too old and had already spent too much time in school, but I also knew that I had some making up to do. So off Doris and I went, third class, on the *Veendam,* a worn-out Dutch tub that, despite its antiquity, provided us a luxurious ten days at sea before we arrived in Holland, where we would live for three and a half years.

We supported ourselves by working together at translating several of the theological works of my mentor, the Dutch theologian Gerrit Berkouwer. Any self-respecting translator is master of the language he is translating from as well as the language he is translating to; I learned the Dutch language by translating it into English. In a couple of years I was able to translate almost as fast as I could type, and before I was finished, I had translated a dozen Dutch books into English.

Before the war, Dutch Reformed theology had become a bare and brittle bone. Defining and redefining the theological formulae left over from meatier days was about all that was left for theologians to do. Then the Nazis came and began shipping Dutch Jews to concentration camps to the east. Along with the few communists in Holland, the Dutch Calvinists formed the backbone of resistance. And nobody who lived through the terrors of the time could ever again ask the big questions about God in the calm old way.

The Reformed Churches would never be the same. They had shared the suffering of the Jews and in their suffering rediscovered themselves — not as Dutch Calvinists, but as fellow human beings. A decade after Holland had been liberated, Berkouwer came to lecture in the United States. When he had finished one of his lectures, someone in the audience asked him: "How do you account for the radical change in Dutch theology?" His answer was: "The Jews."

In Amsterdam, I spent two and a half years in our garret apartment poring over European theology past and present until I was prepared to take the doctoral exam. The exam was done in two parts. The first part, for which male students wore formal cutaways, was an oral exam before five professors. The second part required the student to write a mini-dissertation on a topic assigned to him if he survived the first part. For this task, he was given five days to study and write and then deliver by bicycle a copy of the mini-dissertation to each of the five professors, whose homes were scattered around the city of Amsterdam. This, mind you, was back when scholars wrote their books without the benefit of computers and students wrote and copied their papers without the benefit of copying machines.

I was assigned to write my mini-dissertation on the very question that had so puzzled me when I, in seminary, wrote about Athanasius. Athanasius's strange fourth-century argument for the full deity of Christ was that Jesus had to be God because if he were not God he would not have been able to make us gods. I wrote that we can understand Athanasius only if we remember that he was giving a Christian answer to a question that only Greeks and other Easterners would have asked: How can we become immortal? (Which was a variation of the evangelical question: How can we get to heaven?) Since only the gods are immortal, they quite reasonably figured, we mortals must become gods if we also wish to be immortal. And so the question shifts from how we can get to heaven to how we can be deified and thus be immortal.

The examining committee judged that my argument was acceptable and declared me doctorandus — "doctor to be" — which was not a prediction but a license to begin writing an honest-to-goodness dissertation.

Berkouwer then nudged me across the English Channel to read and write about Anglo-Catholics and their theology of the incarnation. In those days, soon after the war, the only theology European scholars considered worth reading was born either in Switzerland or in Germany. British theologians returned the compliment: the only theology a civilized person would want to read was born in Edinburgh or in Oxford. Austin Farrer, a poetic Anglo-Catholic thinker, pretty much captured their feelings about German theology: "When the German theologians roll their eyes and breathlessly say, *Er redet dich an* (God is speaking to you), I am sure they are saying something significant. I am equally sure they are not speaking to my condition."

Berkouwer, however, had a hunch that British thinkers might be speaking to *his* condition. He had always had one ear cocked toward the East, and he knew that some Anglo-Catholics were wrestling with the same issues that Eastern Orthodox theologians had been working on ever since Athanasius. He wanted to know what was being written and said across the Channel and sent me over to find out. My attention, then, would be focused once more on a variation of the question that every Christian theology asks: *Why?* Why did God have to become man?

Classic Protestant theology has always held that God had to become man so that, as one of us, he could suffer the punishment to which God the Father had already sentenced the rest of us. Athanasius's question was not quite the same. He did not merely ask why God became man. He asked why the God who had become human had to be one hundred percent God and not some semi-divinity very close to God. And — as I have written earlier — his answer was this: he had to be fully God because if he were not fully God himself, he could not have made us gods.

Now Anglo-Catholics asked a more practical question: Since we become divine, how and when and where does our deification come about? And what difference does it make for us when it does happen?

In any case, I took the Channel steamer from The Hook of Holland to the port of Harwich and then boarded a train for Oxford to find suitable digs for Doris and me to live in while I looked for the answer. ☙

CHAPTER FOURTEEN

God and I at Oxford

I found our rooms at Mrs. Harris's house. Being a born and bred Cockney, Mrs. Harris called herself Mrs. Ars, with a rolling *r*, and often giggled at our American accent. But she giggled even more when we told her that, in our ears, she had an accent. We had a small sitting room that was more than well heated by a large coal-burning fireplace and a bedroom so cold and clammy that it took a British stiff upper lip to go to bed. We shared Mrs. Harris's small kitchen and her toilet; we reached the latter by walking through her kitchen, out the back door, taking another two left turns through the garden, and arriving at an outhouse attached to the house, but as cold as the inside of a working refrigerator. After every meal Mrs. Ars would look at the ceiling and say out loud as if she were telling the neighbors, "I thank God for my good meal."

Her house was packed into a row of identical red brick working people's houses. Since most of the houses had more than one fireplace, they also had more than one chimney. So when Doris arrived after dark and caught a glimpse of all the chimneys, she was tickled at the prospect of living smack amid the "spires of Oxford."

I did a good bit of my research at Oxford's grand Bodleian Library, where, on registering, I had to solemnly swear that I would not set the place on fire. In those days, the Bodleian scorned any technology that might speed up the getting of books; if a reader arrived at nine and got the book she needed before ten, she could take it as a sign that the day ahead would be a good one. No books ever left the library, which closed at five. So I used the evenings to read the novels of Fyodor Dostoyevsky, which were to be more important to my life with God than any single theological work that I have since read; no theological system could expose the complications and contradictions of the human spirit so vividly or demonstrate the mercy of God so powerfully as did this greatest of all Russian novelists.

Oxford scholars, as a class, tended to be either shy or curt or both. The superb Austin Farrer lectured with his back turned to the five of us who attended, while his fingers fiddled with a door knob. Then there was J. N. D. Kelly, the author of two celebrated books about the creeds and doctrine of the early church. I was all but mesmerized by his lectures on how the Holy Trinity had survived the scurvy disputes about it during the fourth century, the champion being, of course — and right down my alley — St. Athanasius.

I had been working one day at the Bodlean Library and when five o'clock, quitting time, came around, Dr. Kelly and I reached the door at the same time. Ah, thought I, maybe, if I ask him, he will let me walk to his apartment with him. I asked him. More because he was trapped than as a freely offered invitation, he muttered, yes. Getting in step with him, he under his umbrella and I under mine, I jumped right into his subject, the Holy Trinity. First I asked him about a contemporary Anglo-Catholic, L. S. Thornton, who had recently written a huge volume about the Trinity. "Tried to read it, far too difficult for me," he muttered. And that was that. I tried again. What about William Temple, the great Archbishop of Canterbury, who back in the nineteenth century had devised a social theory about the Trinity? "Don't know a d****** thing about it; I'm a fourth-century man." That too was that. Good night, Dr. Kelly.

But, for curtness, it was hard to beat C. S. Lewis when he was present at his legendary Socratic Club. Forget about suffering fools gladly, he did not suffer very intelligent people gladly. If someone asked him a dumb question, Lewis would snap his head off. To call him churlish would, I think, exaggerate his impatience, but only slightly; anything less than quick brilliance got short shrift from the beloved author of all those wonderful children's books.

The gentle Oxford philosopher Michael Foster was another sort of man. I was a guest once at lunch in the senior commons of Christ Church and I sat next to him; he was the only person who noticed that I was there and made me feel very welcome. A tender, outgoing man, he made lively conversation with me. But he went home one night and — for reasons nobody seemed to know — turned on his gas oven, put his head in it, and died.

I often worked, mostly with my hands inside mittens, at the library of Pusey House, an unheated stone cloister where monks and scholars lived and worked and worshipped. The house was named after Edward Bouverie Pusey, who had been a famous biblical scholar of the nineteenth century and had played a leading role in the Tractarian Movement, which, in its turn, nourished the new form of Anglicanism called Anglo-Catholicism. Pusey House is the world's depository of its literature. When I was there, his library was open to scholars of Anglo-Catholicism — both men and women.

It was here that Doris and I were thrown out of church. Pusey House was established, a dark sign above the door said, for Oxford men to combine their scholarly pursuits with a monastic sort of life. The chapel was long and narrow, with one center aisle and only one entrance, which was at the front of the sanctuary just to the right of the altar. A notable Anglo-Catholic scholar, Dr. F. L. Cross, was to give the homily at the chapel of Pusey House that Sunday, and Doris and I were set on worshipping there.

We arrived barely in time. The chapel was packed and there were no ushers, so we hustled to the rear, where we found room for two in the last pew. We kneeled, said a prayer, and waited for the service to begin. As soon as we had gotten seated, a gaunt, bald gentleman wearing a black gown came bustling down the center aisle toward the rear with his eyes, we felt, fixed on us. When he arrived at our row, he signaled to us with his curved right index finger that he wanted us to come to him. We guessed that he had sized us up as visitors and wanted to take us to a better seat nearer the pulpit and the altar. But when we had gotten within earshot of him he whispered, "You must leave at once, before the mass begins. Women are not permitted to worship in this chapel." The library, but not the chapel, of Pusey House was open to women.

Anglo-Catholicism was a sort of sacramental fundamentalism. It resisted any modernizing trends in the Anglican church and was bent on restoring the Church of England to its ancient Catholic doctrines and worship. Like other fundamentalists, Anglo-Catholics believed that their beliefs were the only right beliefs and that their high-church liturgy was the only right way for Christians to worship.

For an Anglo-Catholic, the pivot around which all of Christian life turned was the incarnation of the Son of God. Christmas, not Good Friday, was the big day on their calendar. To them, the incarnation was not an event in which God emptied himself of divinity, came down to earth, and became a man. It was the event in which God stayed where he was and elevated the humanity of Christ to divinity.

Saving grace was not only God's forgiveness of human sinners, it was a divine energy that lifts humanity into divinity,
its final boost into the final stage of its evolution.

I was sure that when Anglo-Catholics talked this way
they were saying something very significant. I also knew
that they were not talking to my condition. I had never felt a
need to be deified. To be forgiven, loved, and accepted was
what I needed. I was, top to bottom, a Westerner and I simply did not know how to imagine my experience of grace as
my deification. ✦

CHAPTER FIFTEEN

Attracted to Rome

B efore going to Oxford I was studying Protestant theology during the years following the Reformation as it declined step by step from a magnificent creation into a collection of precise definitions. Protestant theologians splintered the Protestant churches with the making of each new definition of mysteries that cannot be defined. One leader after another would get his own slant on certain doctrines, and, when others refused to see the light as he did, would begin a new church. I wondered: Did the Reformation turn every religious leader into a shrunken Pope? And did it give every splinter group the go-ahead to call itself the one Holy Catholic Church? And I began to wonder whether the church of Christ would not have been better off if Luther had never posted his famous theses or the Pope had had enough wisdom to leave him alone.

(Dutch Reformed people carried their separatist streak with them when they immigrated, and, now and then, carried it to an extreme length. When I was a parish minister, I came across a group of three Dutch families in Paterson, New Jersey, who had joined together to form what they believed to be the only true Christian church in America. But they had a disagreement. And, finding no way to resolve it, they split into two churches, one with two and the other with one family, each sure that it was the only truly Christian church in America.)

On a drowsy Oxford Sunday afternoon, Doris and I were strolling down Broad Street and noticed a small cluster of people at the foot of the Martyrs' Memorial that had been erected to honor Thomas Cranmer, Hugh Latimer, and Nicholas Ridley, all Protestant leaders who had fallen afoul of Catholic politics and been burned at the stake. That afternoon three Catholic evangelists, spokespersons for the Catholic Evidence League — two of them lay persons, and the other a priest — were speaking in turns from a portable platform they had set up alongside the statues of the Protestant martyrs. I do not remember what their topic of the day was, but I remember that when they explained a particular Roman Catholic dogma, they would say that "*the* church teaches." Or they would say "*we* believe," as if their "we" were the whole of Christendom. So when they invited questions from the audience, I challenged their pretensions.

"You keep telling us what *the* church believes when, in fact, you are telling us what the *Roman Catholic Church* believes. And you keep saying '*We* believe,' as if all Christians believed what you believe. Wouldn't it be more honest if, instead of saying 'We believe,' you say 'the Roman Catholic Church believes'?"

My remark touched off a lively debate. More and more Sunday strollers stopped, and they soon became a crowd big enough to warm the heart of any itinerant evangelist. It was three against one, but I held my own for a while before I made a really stupid mistake: I began using the same language they did. They would keep saying, "We believe," and I would say, "But we believe." They had me. "Who is your 'we'?" they wanted to know. "Is it the Lutherans? Or maybe the Methodists, or Baptists, or Pentecostals? Just who is your 'we'?" Good question, I thought, who is my "we"?

When Doris and I had finished in Oxford and were back in Holland, I continued to stew about the "we" question until I had almost persuaded myself to seek out a priest, take instruction, and become Roman Catholic. But then a bunch of down-to-earth practicalities began to swamp my idealism. When would I make the move? What if Doris should not want to come along? Since, being married, I could not become a priest, what would I do for a living? What would my mother think? And could I really live with my conscience if I had to accept whatever the Pope said about some of the most fundamental issues of life?

One night our friend Miklos Toth came over for dinner. Miklos was a wan Hungarian who was at the time studying international law in Amsterdam. As the talk went on, I told him about my inclinations. He waited for me to finish, and then he asked me: "What is it that you are looking for? Comfort? Or Truth?"

I had to admit that comfort was what I wanted. I wanted the same comfort that John Henry Cardinal Newman (who had made a huge stir when he left the Anglican for the Roman Catholic Church) had found when, once he accepted the infallibility of the Pope, all his doubts evaporated. I too wanted the comfort of knowing that when the chips were down, somebody with ultimate credibility would settle the issue for all of us. And I wanted the comfort of knowing that my "we" was not just one of a swarm of sects, but a family of faith with bloodlines reaching back to Christ and with arms reaching around the world.

I remained a Protestant, but not because I had at the last moment remembered Rome's famous heresies and twisted practices. The Catholic Church was different after Vatican II; if the church of Martin Luther's day had been anything like it was in the days of John XXIII, when I was flirting with it, the Protestant Reformation would most probably never have occurred. What pulled me away from Rome was my memory of a covenant I had made with my own small church; its history had become my history, its creeds had become my creeds, and its people had become my people. So I recommitted myself to my small and fractious church, which, when it started, chose to call itself, in a touching moment of modesty, the *Christian* Reformed Church.

Some years later I found myself in a monthly conversation between Reformed and Catholic theologians and philosophers. At the close of one of our evenings, an elderly Dominican philosopher came to me and said: "I can tell by what you say and how you say it that in your heart of hearts you should be a Catholic; I dearly wish you really were."

"But I am catholic," I said.

"Oh yes, I know what you mean, but I shall pray for your conversion the rest of my life."

I think she did. ✢

CHAPTER SIXTEEN

God and I in Basel

When the day came for me to defend my dissertation publicly, I was so frightened that I could barely carry myself over the canal bridges I needed to cross to get to the academic hall. I knew for sure that this time I would be exposed as an academic imposter. Once inside, I stood on a small platform resembling the dock in a British courtroom where the accused stands to face the music. On my left side sat the robed, hooded, and frowning faculty; in front of me sat assorted friendly guests. My two paranymphs, elegant in tails and striped pants, stood, each at one side of me, ready to hand me a book or two if I needed them.

The first of the faculty to question me almost undid me by prefacing his question with an untraditionally encouraging word: "Before I offer my challenge," he said, "I want to thank you from my heart for this beautiful dissertation." Getting my bearings again after this dear man's amazing grace, I settled down to field the challenges as best I could in the Dutch language. When the *Pedel* — a sort of academic warden — finally cried out, *Hora Est* ("Time is up"), the faculty adjourned to another room, chatted over a cup of tea, and filed back in to announce that by the power bestowed upon them by her royal highness Queen Juliana, they had agreed to honor me with a degree. We all then retired to a reception room where they and my guests, following hoary custom — and at my expense — nibbled Dutch dainties, smoked Dutch cigars, drank Dutch gin, and became more and more convivial as the gin settled in.

Before I had finished in Amsterdam, Doris had gone home to America to earn us a little start-up money. So, by myself, I took the Rhine Express down to Basel, where I hoped to spend a month listening to Karl Barth, a man most theologians still consider the most important theologian since the Reformation. I arrived in Basel late in the afternoon, located an attic room whose amenities went no further than a hot plate and a small pan for heating water and boiling sausages, and then walked over to the university to find out when and where the great one would be lecturing.

The first person I met was a South African student who, it turned out, was Barth's assistant and, when needed, his personal caretaker. A fellow Calvinist, he was eager for me to come under Barth's influence, and, to make sure that I did, he told me when and where I could hear him, beginning that very night when Barth would be conducting his weekly seminar for English-speaking students.

After his seminars, Barth usually walked over to a small

café for a glass of wine and some talk with a few of his students. It was my new friend's job to guide the aging professor back to his home on the Pilgrimstrasse, so he invited me to come along with the privileged group. So there I was, on my very first night in Basel, a nobody, drinking Rhine wine and chatting with *der Grösse*. I did this for two nights each week during the month I stayed in Basel.

Since Barth set the agenda, I expected on that first night to be party to the theological conversation of a lifetime. But on this night we talked mostly about American cold-war politics, which Barth thought were a dangerous folly, and about great men of the church who had died while sitting on the toilet, among them Luther, Erasmus, and Arius the *bête noire* of Athanasius.

Next time out, however, we talked serious theology and my South African friend maneuvered us onto the subject of universalism. The old-fashioned Enlightenment view of human destiny was that the God of Jesus was too benign to send anyone, and that human beings were too noble to be sent, to eternal damnation. Conservative evangelical theologians feared that Barth was tilted toward the belief that all members of the human family will be saved. My friend wanted me to get the truth straight from Barth himself.

He egged Barth on until the folksy theologian fairly sizzled, put his face a few inches from mine, and crackled, *Ich bin kein universalist* ("I am no universalist")! But he was not finished with me. He poked his finger into my chest and said to me: "You believe the Bible? Fine, then believe this verse too," and he quoted St. Paul, who said that Christ had died "not for our sins only, but for the sins of the whole world." "If you are so worried about universalism," Barth continued, "you had better begin worrying about the Bible."

I felt privileged to have been the personal target of Barth's anger. But I did not really need it, because, in fact, I had been much impressed by his vision of a divine grace coming so triumphantly from the cross of Christ that our puny NO to God cannot stand up against God's loving YES to us.

But is it true? The Bible, in various places, says that we can get to heaven only if we believe in Jesus Christ. If we do not believe in him, we are to be condemned to a lake of fire. Does this horrible future await the millions of people who lived before Christ was born? Does it include those who have suffered under human abuse so shattering that they are not able even to comprehend a simple sentence like "God loves you"? On the other side of the fence, what about people who were forced to believe at the point of a sword? Does their forced faith assure them a place in heaven?

I do not believe that any of us is good enough to buy a seat in heaven with the small coins of our virtue. It seems to me that good and evil are so hopelessly tangled through all of our spirits that none of us could get through the security gates of heaven without a pass. I believe that God will, in some way that I cannot imagine, judge people both for refusing his love and for abusing his children. So my hope is based neither on God's soft heart nor on our moral virtue.

Come to think of it, I have a hunch that I would be put out if certain notoriously evil people ended up nestled in the bosom of the Savior. Something in me does not want Nero, Hitler, Stalin, and the other monsters of history to share the joys of heaven with St. Francis and Mother Teresa. My moral sense demands that God require an accounting from them.

And yet? Suppose we found Stalin's diary and read his last entry: "I repent of my horrible sins. I am the chief of sinners. But I have met Jesus Christ and cling to him as my Savior. Praise the Lord, he promised to forgive me, even me, all of my most grievous sins." Would we not be thankful that Christ can save the meanest and worst of all sinners? Even if, like the thief on the cross, he became a believer a few hours *before* he died?

Now imagine that he had not repented at all before he died, but that a few hours *after* he died, he was struck down by the light of God's blinding grace and glory, and that when he had gotten his sight back, he said to Jesus: "I am the chief of sinners, the worst of them all, judge me, damn me as I deserve." And imagine that Jesus said to him: "I have already judged you and found you guilty. But I am willing to forgive even your most grievous sins." Would it make very much difference if, instead of being saved just *before* he died, he was saved just *after* he died?

I cannot be sure. I do not have the faith to *believe* that Stalin can be saved. And yet I can *hope* that all people will be saved. In fact, I cannot *not* hope for it. My hope is a spirit's wish, a mind's dream, and a heart's faith that it never pays to underestimate the mercy of God. ⨙

CHAPTER SEVENTEEN

God and I in Paterson

When Doris and I came home from Europe, I was called to be the pastor of a small congregation in Paterson, New Jersey, located in a rundown section of that rundown town, doing nobody in the needy neighborhood much good. People in the neighborhood returned the compliment by paying no notice at all to our cozy little brick church hibernating on Madison Avenue near Tenth.

I was called to lead this faithful group of Sunday visitors into a new identity as a "live-in" servant *of* the community. But I had been spending my time in Europe thinking deep thoughts about God and did not have a single practical notion of how a church of commuters could be transformed into a neighborhood ministry of grace. I failed.

I dreamt the dream, however, and others more savvy and gifted than I was, eventually made the dream come true. The little church that nobody noticed back then is now the control center of a ministry for all the needs of all the people in the area who need help of whatever kind. And the small group of white worshippers that I once served has become a many-colored community that every day does more — in proportion to its size — for needy people than any other church I know.

During my days in Paterson, and precisely on the challenge of being a multiethnic community, I experienced my biggest disappointment with my denomination. It so happened that a small Christian Reformed church, struggling to thrive in a small village in the center of North Carolina, was intimidated by its neighbors into turning away a family of color from its worship and from its school. I was sent south to size up the situation and come back with some recommendations. When I came back, I drafted a statement that declared to the world that our denomination was ready to open its doors and its membership to all people of whatever color. Our regional assembly approved of it and sent it on to the General Synod.

The General Synod rejected it. Before a vote was taken, the elders of the assembly reminded us "young idealists" that integration of black people into our church would never work because our doctrines were too deep and rich for them to comprehend. To this insult, they tried to revive a dead notion that both the Bible and tradition support the separation of races in the church as well as in society. And, as the *coup de grace*, they warned that if we took "them" into our church we would eventually end up with "them" as wives and husbands of our children.

I was baffled, ashamed, furious, and was not much placated by the excuse that the time was not yet ripe for integration. Or that in a church so fearful of change as ours was, we should not expect change so soon. Things, thank God, are different now; today, we are as integrated as most any church is, which, though not saying much, does say something.

One of my more peculiar challenges as a pastor in Paterson was to keep myself from vomiting on sick people while I comforted them on their hospital beds. The hospitals I visited were mostly for poor, nonpaying patients. There were no private rooms; people were put up in wards of ten or fifteen beds, and the most distinctive feature of these wards was a sickening odor that left no stomach at peace with itself, least of all mine. Every Wednesday, visiting day, before I got out of my rusted Plymouth, I laid my forehead on the steering wheel and prayed fervently that the Maker of the Universe would reach down from heaven to calm my stomach and keep me from vomiting on patients while I was bending over them and praying for their souls.

After I visited my ailing parishioner, I would do the rounds of the other patients in the ward, each of whom was on a lonely slide to certain death. I remember one man named Jan, who had deserted his family in the Netherlands years before, put out to sea on a freighter, and never came back. Now he was dying — alone — of lung cancer. One afternoon he told me that he had given his heart to Jesus, that he wanted me to conduct his funeral, and that he wanted to be buried in his only suit, which I would find inside a piece of luggage that he had left with the owner of a diner where in his better days he had eaten most of his meals. The diner was in the city of Prospect Park; the owner's name was George. The next time I came, Jan was dead.

He had not given me much to go on, so I did the only thing that I could think of. I drove over to Prospect Park — a city with roughly 80,000 citizens — to see if I could find a man named George who ran a diner. I turned off the freeway into a residential part of the town, and on the first block I spotted a man sprinkling his front lawn. Since I had to begin somewhere, I figured that I may as well begin with him. I parked nearby and walked over to him.

"I am looking for a man named George who runs a diner in this town. Can you help me?"

"Yeh," he said. "My name is George and I run a diner."

I told him that Jan had died. I was a minister, I explained, and wanted to get some clothes for him to be buried in. George recalled that Jan had indeed left a suitcase at the diner. But George wavered. How did he know what was in that suitcase or why I was so eager to get my hands on it? Maybe it held a bundle of ill-gotten cash. But after a bit of talk, I convinced him that I was a legitimate minister, and he led me into the house and to the kitchen, where his wife, a cordial, chubby woman, was at her gas stove making his dinner. George left me with her while he went up to the attic for the suitcase.

It was a hot day, and she was wearing a fluffy apron tied around a summery cotton dress. When George had gone up to the attic to get the suitcase she turned around with her back to the stove and began to chat with me. That was when she caught on fire. Before she went up in smoke before my eyes, I swung her around and began beating her ample backside with both of my hands. As I was swatting her behind, George appeared in the kitchen with the suitcase in his hand.

The next day I presided over Jan's funeral. Besides myself and the organist, there were two women present, both strangers to me. When I later told a few of my parishioners what had happened, one of them told me it must have been God who led me to George the diner man. I was skeptical. What with the whole world on his hands, would God care that much about whether Jan had his dress-up suit on when he went to his grave? Did he have time to stretch his arms down to Prospect Park and nudge George to sprinkle his lawn just as I came looking for him? I don't know. But I thanked God anyway for helping me out.

Some of my best parishioners were offspring of a Calvinistic group in the Netherlands that specialized in bewailing their sinfulness. They were kin to the Dutch farmers who, during the great flood of 1953, refused to be rescued from their floating housetops on the grounds that if God saw fit to send a flood as punishment for their sins, they had no business trying to escape. Their forebears worshipped in barns and listened every Sunday to men of God haranguing them for their sin and misery. One Sunday morning when the preacher got himself into an inspired frenzy of judgment, five women broke out wailing and howling for their grievous sins. The preacher ordered the five of them to stop their bawling. Three of the women became quiet, the other two kept on howling. At that, the minister told his people to bow their heads as he prayed: "I thank thee, Lord, that thou hast this day exposed three hypocrites among us."

More than a few of the people in my church were of a similar spirit. It would, they thought, be sinfully presumptuous for them to assume that they had the credentials of genuine Christians. If asked whether they did not consider themselves to be Christians, they would say: "Oh no, we are not good enough to boast that we are Christians, but we hope to be." What they hoped for was that, on their deathbeds, God himself would come in a pure shaft of white light and give them the blessed assurance that it was, after all, well with their souls.

I made more than my share of mistakes at Madison Avenue, mistakes which, if they were ever aware of them, the good people I worked for were quick to forgive. But there was one mistake I made early on that was all but unforgivable. I forgot that the worshippers whom I was called to serve were ordinary people — not leaders, not educated, not wealthy, just working people — and would never be anything else. I wanted them to be leaders, visionaries, educated, wealthy, and in my heart I faulted them for not fitting my notion of what I wanted them to be. Then I remembered what my former professor of church history told me the night that I was ordained. Walking into the church with him, I asked him if he had one last piece of advice for me. "Yeh," he said, "just remember that the people of your church are ordinary people. If you take them as they are, you will do OK."

I did sometimes forget that I was called to serve *these* people, not the elite Christians that I wished they were. When I did forget, I was ineffective, unloving, impatient, wretched. As time went by, however, and as I learned more about myself, I knew that I was just as weak, just as limited, just as insecure, just as boring, just as frightened — and just as sinful — as they were. When I finally got that fact firmly lodged in my soul, I became, I think, a passable servant. ✣

CHAPTER EIGHTEEN

Back Again at Calvin College

After a few years as a parish minister, I was invited by the Calvin College Board of Trustees to become a teacher of religion and theology at the college, where as a student I had discovered the Calvinist faith. Now, for us Calvinists, right *thinking* about God is as important as right *experience* of God is for Pentecostals. So when the Board asked me to teach theology at its college, it was investing a major trust in me — not so much to teach mere truth as to teach its truth, its Reformed truth, indeed, its Dutch Reformed truth. I accepted the appointment.

I could scarcely take it in that I was now a colleague of the same teachers I had almost worshipped when I was a student. I tried every day to silence a demon whose voice sounded a lot like my mother's and who kept telling me that I was not smart enough to work alongside these great teachers and that I would before long be exposed. But I gave it my best effort and soon knew for sure that being a teacher was all I ever could want to be and that being a teacher at Calvin was grace abounding.

Calvin students were not, like those at Yale or Harvard, the pick of the academic litter. But what they lacked in scholastic achievement, they made up for in Calvinistic seriousness. I loved them — sappy as it may sound, I loved those young people. What is more, I loved teaching the Bible and theology.

Several theological follies danced on the American stage during the decade that I taught theology at Calvin. Some of them seemed like theological shilly-shally to me at the time, especially the one that came to be known as the "Death of God" theology. It was, I thought, an opportunity for its champions to have the fifteen minutes of fame that everybody is supposed to have coming, but not much more. If anyone had died, I figured, it could not have been God. And if he was God, he could not have died. That was easy. But then I realized that the "death of God" was a theatrical and perhaps desperate way of accounting for where God was while Hitler was savaging Europe. The answer was that either God had died and was not around to prevent the holocaust or that the holocaust killed God. It was my kind of question, just not my kind of answer.

A more sophisticated notion of God came from what we still call "Process Theology." God, according to this theology, as I understood it, is in process, not yet ripe, not come of age, and our expectations of him should take his immaturity into account. If we get discouraged with God, we should remember that, as gods go, our God is still minor league, almost but not quite ready for the majors. He is still growing in tempo with the expanding universe. He cannot get out in front of the universe for the simple reason that he is still emerging from the universe. If there were no universe, there would be no God; God minus the universe equals nothing.

I would rather have my problems with the God who created the world than solve my problems by trading him in for a God who is being created by the world. I cannot let God off the hook of human suffering by making believe he is not yet a grown-up God. I would rather deal with a God who was there, full-grown and ready to take charge, the moment he had gotten the good world made. For me, if there were no God, there would be no universe; the universe minus God equals God.

Earlier, when I talked about how I became a member of the Christian Reformed Church, I described some of the leaders in the church as people of the gap and others as people of the bridge. By the gap I meant a spiritual ravine between the mind of Reformed Christians and the mind of unbelievers and liberals. The gap people wanted to build walls along the edge of the ravine to protect the innocent from the lure of the siren songs they heard coming from the other side. The bridge people wanted to build bridges across the gap so that they could cross over and reap the benefits of contact with the people on the other side. While I taught at Calvin, the gap people and the bridge people spoke their minds in their journals. The gap folks published *Torch and Trumpet,* which, for the most part, was a call to arms. The bridge people published *The Reformed Journal,* which the editors considered to be a call to dialogue.

After a time, I was invited to join the editorial staff of *The Reformed Journal,* and I was sure that no other honor could ever match this one; my co-editors were all my intellectual and spiritual heroes, and to join their company was, I thought, about as good as it would ever get. The best part of being their colleague was the monthly staff meeting. One of the blessings of those meetings was my discovery that my heroes were men of common clay, just as I was. I learned that we all had shared the human tendency to distort reality in order to make us feel better about it. We tended, for instance, to exaggerate the importance of the crises to which we responded, and we also tended to see the folly and vice of our critics as evidence of our own wisdom and virtue. We all smoked cigarettes in those days and shamelessly befouled the air of the homes at which we met. Smoking was the one bad thing I learned to do at Calvin!

The most exciting, maybe bizarre, thing that happened while I was one of the *Journal* editors was the McIntire affair. In the years of cold-war politics, a Senator by the name of Joseph McCarthy was furiously exposing supposed communists in the government; about the same time, a Christian minister by the name of Carl McIntire was — on his daily radio show — furiously exposing supposed communist sympathizers in the church. Both of them represented what we called the Far Right. The *Journal* took the occasion of the times to devote an issue to the Far Right in America. I wrote a piece critical of McIntire. He read it and rose up in wrath against me.

He along with many others. I had never received hate mail before, but now I was avalanched by it, and I discovered just how crazy it could be. The whole fuss brought out the very best in Calvin's leadership. Its president, William Spoelhof, made no complaint to *The Reformed Journal* about the trouble we had caused him; instead, he invited McIntire to come to Calvin, speak in our chapel, and tell us face to face what was wrong with us. He came and fiercely indicted all of us, especially me, as threats to true religion and American freedom. But he was treated with courtesy, and when his harangue was finished he was cordially wished a safe trip back to New Jersey. What impressed me most about the showdown with McIntire was the poised leadership that President Spoelhof exhibited that day. His poise reassured me that Calvinism was a faith with guts, and with wisdom to go along with them. ✧

CHAPTER NINETEEN

Common Grace

Souring the joy I had in my teaching was an old and rancorous controversy of the kind that could occur only in the belly of a Dutch Calvinistic community. As most everyone knows, one of the tenets of Calvinist faith is the belief that God elected certain sinners (whom he had yet to create) to be died for by his Son and to live with him happily forever. But the prickly part is that he chose not to save any of the others. They were rejected out of hand, even while they existed only in God's imagination. Those whom he left out, and who therefore were damned, we call the reprobate.

Now it is obvious that God gives the reprobate many wonderful gifts — moral character, intelligence, creativity, and sometimes a lot of money. The question was, why? Why does he give such good things to the very people whom he has already marked for damnation?

Some Calvinists believe that when God gives good gifts to reprobates, he is really giving them no grace at all. What he gives them is — in disguise, of course — a golden rope to hang themselves with. God knows ahead of time, and actually sees to it that the reprobates will not be thankful to him for the gifts he gives them and will, in fact, use the gifts for their own selfish ends. So when God gives good gifts to reprobates, he is not being gracious to them at all; he is only fattening them up for the kill.

Other Calvinists believe that when God gives good things to people whom he has already damned, he is genuinely feeling gracious toward them. But the grace he gives them is not the amazing grace that "saves a wretch like me." It is a common grace; it is given indiscriminately to all sinners, the reprobate right along with the elect. This grace does not get the reprobates to heaven; it only makes their doomed lives in the waiting room of damnation a bit more pleasant and much more useful.

For many years, the notion of common grace softened the edges of the brutal doctrine of reprobation for me. It told me that God wants us to enjoy the graces that gifted people offer us without worrying about whether they came from reprobate sinners. So I could thank God for giving Mozart the grace to write his flute concertos, for giving Plato the wisdom that led some early Christians to believe that he had borrowed it from Moses, and for giving Arthur Miller the grace to write marvelous plays like *The Death of a Salesman*. All of them I could admire regardless of whether they were among the elect or among the reprobate.

Yet, I sometimes wondered. If God *really* wanted to be

gracious toward reprobate sinners, why didn't he just call off their reprobation? And if these people were damned before they had drawn a breath, are they getting much of a favor when God gives them nice gifts to make their rush to hell a tad less horrible? It made the gifts of common grace seem too much like the choice meal murderers get before they are strapped to an electric chair. Some gift! Some grace!

This leaves me with a still tougher question: How can kind and gentle Christians actually believe that God would do such a horrible thing as damn people before they had a chance to earn their damnation? The only way to explain how good people could keep swallowing such bad doctrine is to link it to what they think was God's reason for creating a world in the first place.

John Calvin and all his successors have agreed that God created a world so that he could get glory and honor for creating it. It was as if God looked at his own perfection and, wonderful as it was, he was sorry that there was no one beside himself to admire it and praise him for it. So he created a beautiful world and then created people who could praise him for creating it.

Anyone who accepts the notion that God's main motive for creating the universe was to receive honor and glory from the elect and reprobate is disqualified from judging what he does to get it. Suppose a candidate for the presidency of the United States told us that he wanted to be president only for the honor and the glory that it would bring. If we approved of his motives, we would not be in a position to criticize the methods he used to get elected. So with God. If his own glory — even if it were the glory of his love — was what he was after, who are we mortals to wince if he goes to some deplorable extremes to get it?

It seems to me now that God must have wanted to create a world for the same reason that he wanted to redeem it. The gospel tells us very clearly why he wanted to redeem the world: God sent his Son, not to condemn the world, but to save it. And he wanted to save it for one simple reason: he loved it. Now, if love is why he wants to fix the world, love must be the reason he made it in the first place.

Mind now, I am sure that God is thrilled when anyone looks at the "purple mountain majesty" of our earth and breaks out with a "Glory be to God." And thrilled too when a saved sinner lifts his hands and sings "Amazing Grace." But, it seems to me that we make God out to be an absolute narcissist — someone who loves only himself — when we say that his main motive for creating the world was to get glory and honor for himself. It simply must be that he created us in order to love us, all of us, and all of us with the same love.

There is no such thing, it seems to me now, as a second-class, or common, grace. God's grace can never be common, never second rate. It is always special. Always amazing. I now believe that the whole idea of an inferior grace for reprobates was something dreamed up to make the doctrine of reprobation seem a mite less horrible than it is. If we stop insulting God by ascribing such a dark doctrine to him, we will have no need of any "common grace." We will have only the one marvelous grace of God for all humankind. What all this comes down to is this: The most glorious thing about God is that he made us not so that we could give him glory, but that he could give us love. And that great love leads him to be gracious to all. ✦

CHAPTER TWENTY

In the Shadow of Death

About four years into our Calvin decade, Doris gave birth to a beautiful baby boy who died before he had lived the whole of a day. God's face has never looked the same to me since. Since my conversion to Calvinism, his face had had the unmovable serenity of an absolute sovereign absolutely in control of absolutely everything. Every good thing, every bad thing, every triumph, every tragedy, from the fall of every sparrow to the ascent of every rocket, everything was under his silent, strange, and secretive control. But I could not believe that God was in control of our child's dying.

It was not as if I had found a forgotten Bible verse or saw a familiar one in a new light. It was more like something that happened to me when I was fifteen, hitchhiking through Georgia, waiting at the docks for a ride with a trucker. I heard a young white man curse an aging black man who had gotten in his way, cussed him out with God-rattling oaths; and what is more, he did it in front of the old man's friends. I had never known a black person. I had *never* before seen racism in action. But when I heard its words and saw its face on that early morning in Atlanta, Georgia, I knew for sure that racism was a terrible thing.

That's how I knew for sure that God did not micro-manage our baby's death. I had been intellectually excited by John Calvin's tough-minded belief that all things — and he really meant *all of them,* including the ghastly and the horrible — happen when and how and where they happen precisely as God decreed them to happen. A "horrific decree" Calvin conceded, but if it works out to God's glory, who are we to complain? On the day that our baby boy died, I knew that I could never again believe that God had arranged for our tiny child to die before he had hardly begun to live, any more than I could believe that we would, one fine day when he would make it all plain, praise God that it had happened.

I learned that I do not have the right stuff for such hard-boiled theology. I am no more able to believe that God micro-manages the death of little children than I am able to believe that God was macro-managing Hitler's holocaust. With one morning's wrenching intuition, I knew that my portrait of God would have to be repainted.

I was well aware that every day other people are suffering tragedies infinitely worse than Doris's and mine. And I remembered that I had consoled people whose loss was much greater than ours with the comforting assurance that God knew best. But grief can be a self-centered thing; I had no tears for the wretched and the poor of the earth that day. I had tears only for Doris and myself.

We had spent a decade making love according to a schedule set by four different fertility clinics in three different countries. And finally, after one summer night's lark on the sand dunes of Lake Michigan with no thought but love, Doris became a medically certified pregnant woman.

Six months along and doing fine, we thought — with God answering our prayers it could be no other way but fine — she suddenly one night began losing amniotic fluid. I called her doctor. "She's going into labor," he said. "Get her to the hospital as fast as you can." And then he said he was sorry, but our baby was going to be badly malformed.

"How badly?"

"Very."

We fumbled silent and bewildered into the car. I told her. We cried. And we promised God and each other that we would love the child no matter how damaged she or he was. After Doris had been tucked in, I went to the waiting room to worry for a few hours. Suddenly, Doris's doctor broke in and exulted: "Congratulations, Lew, you are the father of a perfect man-child." I told Doris the news. She was skeptical, but I went home and danced like a delirious David before the Lord.

Next day, just before noon, our pediatrician called: I had better come right down to the hospital. When I met him he told me that our miracle child was dead. Two mornings later, with a couple of friends at my side and our minister reading the ceremony, we buried him "in the sure and certain hope of the resurrection." Doris never got to see her child.

A pious neighbor comforted me by reminding me that "God was in control." I wanted to say to her, "Not this time." It seems to me that the privilege of being the delicate organisms we are in the kind of world we live in comes at a price. The price is that things can go wrong, badly wrong sometimes, which should come as no surprise.

The blossoming of every fleck-like zygote into a humanoid embryo and an embryo into the astounding creature we call a baby is beset with so many threats along the way that any baby who gets delivered into the world as the pride and joy of its mother is nature's most marvelous success story. Every healthy newborn child is a biological miracle; if we did not know that it actually happens every day, we would say that the very notion was a wild man's fantasy.

Doris and I cried a lot and we knew in our tears that God was with us, paying attention to us, shedding ten thousand tears for every one of ours. Neither of us had a moment's inclination to give up on God, to quit believing in him or to quit trusting him. In fact, he never seemed more real to either of us. Never closer. Never more important. I could stop believing that he had micro-managed our tiny boy's dying. But I could not stop trusting that God was still with us.

Four decades later, on the morning of September 11,

2001, Doris and I, with people all over our country, were stunned into silence by the sight of two airliners crashing into the two towers of the World Trade Center in New York City. A gargantuan evil — not a breakdown in physical nature this time, but an evil conceived and willed by human beings. Pure evil does not happen often. Most of the time, evil wears the mask of decency. But this time it wore no mask, and when we saw it, we spelled it with a capital *E*.

It is true that the purity of another's evil does not make our own ways good. But this time, no matter how hard I tried to find one, I could locate no stain in our national behavior dark enough to temper the purity of this evil. What happened that terrible Tuesday was born in the evil intentions of evil men's hearts. The evil of the thing only makes our question the more urgent: Where was God and what was he doing when this evil happened in front of our eyes?

Calvinists seek their answer in the eternal past when God charted the course of every human event. There, in eternity, God wrote the entire script for the whole human drama yet to come. God, not Osama bin Laden, was really in charge when the terrorists murdered all those innocent people. And they have a splendid hymn to comfort them.

> God moves in a mysterious way
>   his wonders to perform.
> He plants his footsteps in the sea
>   and rides upon the storm.

His purposes will ripen fast,
    unfolding every hour.
The bud may have a bitter taste,
    but sweet will be the flower.
Blind unbelief is sure to err
    and scan his work in vain.
God is his own interpreter
    and he will make it plain.

I do not want God to "make it plain." If he could show us that there was a good and necessary reason for such a bad thing to have happened, it must not have been a bad thing after all. And I cannot accommodate that thought. In fact, I have given up asking *why* such bad things happen. Instead, I look to the future and ask *when*. When is God going to come and purge evil from his world? When will he come to make his original dream for the world come true?

For me, there was no mystery about where God was and what he was up to on the morning of September 11, 2001. He was right there doing what he always does in the presence of evil that is willed by men; he was fighting it, resisting it, battling it, trying his best to keep it from happening. This time evil won. God, we hope, will one day emerge triumphant over evil, though, on the way to that glad day, he sometimes takes a beating. ✦

CHAPTER TWENTY-ONE

God and I at Fuller Seminary

O ne early June night in 1968, I had a phone call from Daniel Fuller, then the delightfully diffident dean of Fuller Theological Seminary. After I finished talking with him, Doris asked me what he wanted, and I said that I was not sure but that he seemed to be inviting me to come to California to be a visiting professor at Fuller next year. A second call made it all clear. Edward Carnell, Fuller's former president, had died unexpectedly and the seminary needed someone to replace him temporarily as a professor of theology while they looked for his successor. Doris and the children thought that a year in endless sunshine would be just fine, so I called Dr. Fuller back and told him we would come. And we did.

The beginnings were not all that promising. A week after we had moved into a furnished apartment in Pasadena, John, the youngest of our three adopted children, was diagnosed as having Gaucher's disease, a rather rare genetic blood disease which did not then and does not yet have a cure. During our second week Doris learned that she had breast cancer and would need surgery the week thereafter. She had a radical mastectomy, which was the usual thing to do for breast cancer in those days, but survived it nicely. Meanwhile, I nurtured a selfish pity for myself as I brought the children to their new schools, fed them, tucked them in bed at night, drove to the hospital, and came back too tired to prepare to teach courses that I had never taught before to students who had no idea of what was going on at our house but who came to Fuller with high expectations.

Halfway into my year's visit, I was invited to join the faculty as a tenured member; I accepted and spent the rest of my working days at Fuller, never for a moment hankering to be anywhere else. Among my first happy discoveries at Fuller was its diverse faculty and its even more diverse body of students. My own church supposed that if you want a spiritual community, you had to have theological unity. My experience in a Christian community of individuals whose faith had been nurtured in a dizzying variety of traditions and creeds was a delight to me. A fringe benefit was the freedom to work without ecclesiastical hounds at my heels sniffing for the scent of a theological blooper.

I must admit that I came to Fuller with an arrogance that only partly camouflaged my insecurity. I assumed, for instance, that Pentecostal people were heavy on experience but light on thinking; I very quickly learned that my Pentecostal colleagues were every bit as weighty intellectually as I was. I came with arrogance about my Calvinistic vision of God's redemption not only of individuals, but of the whole world; I soon learned that my colleagues' vision of God's purpose was every bit as grand as my own. I came with the bias that only Calvinists saw beyond personal salvation to social renewal; I very quickly learned that some of my colleagues and most of my students were just as committed to social justice as I was. Being cured of my parochial arrogance was, I believe, one of the very best of the many experiences I had at Fuller, and I treasure the comedown as a gift of God.

Once settled at Fuller, whose inclusive diversity carried with it a certain vulnerability to conflict, I seemed, without trying, to take on a new persona. Within my own circles in the past, I had developed a reputation as a minor-league disturber of Israel. At Fuller I became a conciliator. If a serious controversy broke out and the president appointed a committee to cope with it, you could safely bet that I would be on the committee and often its chairperson. Fuller was founded on the premise that, within the boundaries of evangelical faith, individual differences of insight could only enrich the whole community. But now and then a clash of perspectives within the faculty threatened its unity, and the job of helping to redraw the parameters of freedom was sometimes given to me.

In the eighties, campus gossip buzzed with stories of miracles that were happening on campus in a course known as "Signs and Wonders." The course was meant to be a serious study of the role that miracles have played in the growth of the church, but it got out of control and exploded into a fireworks display of miraculous healings. Word got out and very soon people who had never stepped into a seminary before were lining up to enroll in the course.

My colleagues in theology were worried about reports from around the world that Fuller had become a Pentecostal and charismatic seminary. I was more worried about what it might do to God's reputation than I was about Fuller's reputation. It seemed to me that such healings trivialized God's response to human suffering. I had, for instance, called on God ten thousand times to rescue the 45,000 bruised and battered children who are lost in the Los Angeles County Welfare Department. But, in spite of my prayers, the bruising and the battering went on. I could not believe that the Maker of the Universe would ignore the gargantuan suffering of innocent children, not just in Los Angeles but all over the world, while, at the summons of a charismatic preacher, he would whimsically swoop genie-like into a Fuller classroom to put his healing fingers on a bearable case of bursitis.

We had a splendid new provost at Fuller at that time, and he did what provosts usually do when there is trouble in their faculty: he appointed a task force to study the crisis and advise the faculty. He appointed a task force that included people who were most vigorously for and most vigorously against "Signs and Wonders." He made me its chairman and instructed me to produce a white paper on miraculous healing that would win the approval of the faculty in the fall of the same year

Miraculous healings on campus created the severest test ever of Fuller's ability to function as a community of diverse and often conflicting visions; all of us were nervous. Grace was given me to listen most of the time, and what I heard from my colleagues gradually convinced me that my own image of a God who simply gave nature permission to run its own house needed adjustments. I wrote the paper that summer and presented it to the task force in the early fall; it was unanimously adopted by the task force and by the faculty, and a bit later was published under the title *Ministry and the Miraculous.*

I am more positive about miraculous healing today than I was before "Signs and Wonders." I still believe that God ordinarily allows the creativity and the destructivity of nature to balance things out on their own; we suffer when nature fails us and we heal when nature heals us. But I also now believe that though God usually leaves nature to balance out its own benign and destructive powers, he might — for his own reasons — choose now and then to intrude into the natural balance and bring healing to afflicted people. We should not try to manipulate God into healing action, but we can keep our faith open to the possibility that he might — just might — on occasion take a road less traveled and heal a wound or two on his way. Were I a parish minister today, I would hold healing services in my church regularly.

I had myself had, some years before the "Signs and Wonders" episode, an experience of healing that may have prepared me to open my mind to the possibility that God might, now and then, and at his own discretion, break into the course of nature and heal a person. Five or six years after coming to Fuller (I forget just when), I fell into a depression that made my family's life a misery, turned me into a grouch with my colleagues, made a hash of my relationship with God, and pushed me deep into a dark night of the soul. My experience was, from start to finish, a viper's tangle of resentment toward colleagues, daily lacerations of my own self, a mystery to my family, and a hellish sense that God had abandoned me.

The most fearsome feeling that my craziness set loose in my spirit was a hunch that I was a grotesque hypocrite. Especially when I preached God's grace while I was feeling only God's judgment. I decided that any bona fide preacher needed three spiritual qualities, each of which I lacked. First, he or she must have suffered much: I believed that no one has credentials to preach the gospel of God's Suffering Servant unless he or she had suffered more than most people. Second, a minister must be transparently holy: I believed that only holy men and women were qualified to speak for a holy God. And third, I believed that the gospel fire must be blazing so hot in a preacher's belly that she could not keep her mouth shut if she tried. I did not have even one of the three spiritual qualifications for preaching the gospel. So I tagged myself as unqualified and stopped preaching.

I did not know where God was during this time. I only "knew" that wherever he was, he was not with me. But I was wrong. He was with me because he was in Doris and Doris was with me. What did she do? She did nothing. Nothing but wait. And wait. And wait. God came back to me on the strength of her power to wait for me. Never before had I known the saving power of waiting.

God came back to me at the very moment that I had reached ground zero in my own hopelessness. I had been living alone for a couple of weeks, as a therapeutic regimen, in a secluded cabin on one of the islands in Puget Sound, cut off from all my usual escapes from reality, with no radio or television and no books or magazines that might have given me a few moments' escape from my pain. On the Tuesday afternoon of the third week, while I was pacing the living room floor, I seemed to hear the voices of everyone whose approval I had lived for — my friends, my family, and especially my mother. Each of them came to me in turn and each of them said the same thing: I CANNOT HELP YOU. I felt as if I were sinking into the ocean within arm's reach of a boat full of loved ones who put their arms around their chests and shook their heads as I went down.

Then God came back. He broke through my terror and said: "I will never let you fall. I will always hold you up." When I heard him speak — or, as some of my friends say, imagined that I heard him speak — I felt as if I had been lifted from a black pit straight up into joy. Never before had I been so suddenly released from the devil of despair. Never before had I known such an amazing grace. Never before such elation.

I have not been neurotically depressed since that day, though I must, to be honest, tell you that God also comes to me each morning and offers me a 20-milligram capsule of Prozac. With this medication he clears the garbage that accumulates in the canals of my brain overnight and gives me a chance to get a fresh morning start. I swallow every capsule with gratitude to God. ✦

CHAPTER TWENTY-TWO

The Battle for the Bible

W hen I came to Fuller in 1968, it was a small seminary with about 300 students. By the time I retired
in 1993, it had an enrollment of 4,000 students. This un-
precedented growth was not the work of a talented publicity
office. Neither did it happen because tuition was low and
grants were big; in fact, tuition was high and whatever fi-
nancial aid to students was available, it was too small to be
worth the bother of applying for it. What is more, no students came to Fuller because their denomination expected
them to go there; they were all there because they wanted to
be there.

There are, it seems to me, two reasons for Fuller's phe-
nomenal growth. First, word of its biblical scholarship had
gotten around; it became known that at Fuller scholars tried
to let the Bible — rather than their own dogmatic bias —
tell us the meaning of its message and the method of its dis-
closure. Equally important to its success was its choice of
David Allan Hubbard to be its president.

Hubbard kept the ship on course through the storms of the sixties, the seventies, and the eighties. One of the worst storms was the torching of south-central Los Angeles after a few obviously guilty police officers had been found innocent of beating up a black man. Hubbard responded with a new commitment. Fuller would no longer be a white Protestant theological school. It would be a school devoted to serving the diverse needs of the melting pot called Los Angeles. He invited a large group of Afro-American, Hispanic, and Asian leaders to come and tell us how we could best serve their people. They told us and we listened. Fuller stretched its budget, expanded its services, hired new ethnic leaders, and as a result is probably more truly multi-ethnic than any other theological school in the country.

Another instance of Hubbard's poise in nervous times was his response to an acrimonious book written by a former Fuller dean by the name of Harold Lindsell, who had wanted Fuller to select him rather than Hubbard as its president. He titled his book: *The Battle for the Bible*. The "battle," he said, was about nothing less than the foundation of evangelical faith. The foundation was the doctrine that the Bible neither had nor could have any errors. The stakes were the right to the name of "evangelical." The treacherous enemy was Fuller Seminary, and Lindsell was the self-appointed general leading the charge against God's foe.

But, thanks to David Hubbard, there was no battle. And if there had been a battle, it would not have been about the

Bible. It would have been about Lindsell's fundamentalist *theory* of the Bible. And about whether one had to subscribe to his theory in order to qualify as an honest-to-goodness evangelical Christian. Hubbard was not even tempted to enter a fray on Lindsell's flawed and divisive premises.

Instead, Hubbard invited our faculty to set out the larger and more biblical evangelical agenda. We accepted his invitation and published a large and vigorous declaration of the evangelical mandate for our times. It came to be known as *The Mission Beyond the Mission*. The statement is too long for me to quote here, but a few sentences from the prologue will give an impression of the spirit behind it:

> We must face the tough questions put to us by the Scriptures, the churches, and the contemporary world; we must take the risks necessary to break fresh ground in ministry and broach new ideas in scholarship; we must brave the dangers of our mistakes and the criticism of those who may misunderstand; we must put our biblical convictions into practice, even when the price is high.

I was never so admiring of any academic leader as I was of David Hubbard, and never more thankful to God for the privilege of being a teacher at Fuller than I was when the faculty adopted the document as a statement of our evangelical calling.

Personally, I felt no inclination at all to go into battle

against the shibboleth that one must believe that the Bible contains no errors in order to be considered a bona fide evangelical. The theory — for this is what it was — that the Bible not only was, but had to be, inerrant in order for God to reveal himself through it seems so clearly false to the Bible itself that I could not muster a passion to refute it. And then to turn dispute about this theory into a so-called battle for the Bible seemed to me insulting not to any theologian, but to the God of the Bible himself.

I should, before leaving the subject, explain my own reasons for rejecting the notion that, to be a reliable revelation of God, the Bible may contain no errors of any kind. To begin with, I distinguish roughly between two types of writing in the Bible. One type is what we might call divine poetry. I mean by this the Psalms, the Proverbs, many of its prophetic images and its apocalyptic symbols. The other is what we may call Bible stories, accounts of things God did in the history of the Jews and the story of Jesus.

The poetic books seem obviously not the sorts of writings that any reasonable critic would judge by their literal accuracy. I could not even imagine what anyone could *mean* by saying that the biblical psalms and symbols were "literally inerrant." It is like judging whether a newly discovered painting is a genuine Van Gogh by whether it weighs ten pounds or more. Or evaluating the grandeur of a Beethoven symphony by how long it takes an orchestra to play it.

The Bible's stories are another matter. When it comes to

reporting events of history, the dogma of inerrancy at least makes sense. It makes sense to ask whether the stories in general are free of mistakes. And it makes sense to ask whether any details of the story could be erroneous. The fundamentalist insists that the tellers of these stories did not make, and could not make, a single mistake. If, the fundamentalist claims, we concede that just one of the storytellers has made the tiniest error of fact in the story, we lose our reason for trusting that the story itself is true. And if we cannot trust that any one of the Bible stories is totally without mistakes, neither can we trust the Gospels when they tell the story of Jesus and particularly of his resurrection. The stakes are very high: one error and everything else is cast into the shadow of doubt.

The fundamentalist claim makes sense. But the fact that it makes sense does not make it true. For me, the theory is worse than mistaken; it seems to lay a rather presumptuous limitation on God to insist that God could reveal himself to us only in a book that is totally free of any sort of error.

I will limit my observations to two stories we find in the Gospels. One of them is an episode in the earthly work of Jesus. One writer relates a story of how Jesus healed *two* Gerasene demoniacs, and another writer tells the same story except that in this one Jesus healed just *one* Gerasene demoniac. It seems obvious to me that one of them was mistaken. But for the fundamentalist, neither of them could possibly have made a mistake. Why not? This is why:

If we cannot be sure whether Jesus healed two demoniacs or only one, how can we be sure that he healed any demoniacs at all? And if we cannot be sure whether he healed one demoniac or two, we have lost our confidence in the truth of all four Gospels.

The issue gets a great deal more critical when we come to the stories of Jesus' resurrection. Here the redemption of the world is on the line. Now as one reads the Gospel reports of the resurrection of Jesus, one notices that they differ from one another in certain incidental details of their stories. For instance, two of them (Mark and John) say that only Mary Magdalene went to the tomb and found it empty, after which *an angel* (Mark) or *two* (John) came and talked to them. Another writer (Matthew) tells us that *two* women went to the tomb, Mary Magdalene and Mary the mother of James, and that at the tomb *a young man* appeared to them. Still another writer (Luke) specifies *three* women, Mary Magdalene, Mary the mother of Jesus, and a woman named Joanna (or Salome), and adds, besides, some other, unnamed women. At the tomb, on finding it empty, these women were met by *two men* in shining garments. Discrepancies, only in details to be sure, and none of them affecting the Great Event on which all the writers are as one, but still discrepancies.

The fundamentalist tightens his jaw and growls that no matter how things seem to any unbiased reader, none of the writers could possibly have been mistaken about anything, no matter how incidental. If we allow that even one of them made just one mistake in any detail of the accounts, we have lost all certainty that the whole story is true. And if we allow that the whole story could have been false, the entire ship of faith sinks to the bottom of the ocean. Well, the fundamentalist is right in one thing: if the story of the resurrection were untrue, we would have lost the Christian faith. But the story is true even though those who tell it made some trivial mistakes about what was going on among the amazed and incredulous disciples on Easter morning.

Let me use a parallel situation to illustrate what I have just said. On the morning of September 11, 2001, reporters told us that some five thousand and more people had died when terrorists flew two airliners into the two World Trade Center towers. As the days went by, however, they edited the report to say that only four thousand people died. As more days went by, their number of fatalities was reduced to fewer than three thousand. Now what if someone were to insist that, if on the first day the reporters wrote that X number of people were killed, and on the next wrote that Y number of people were killed, and on the third day wrote that Z number of people were killed, we can no longer be sure that the Twin Towers had actually collapsed at all?

The resurrection of Jesus was an event of infinitely greater surprise and incredulity than the collapse of the Trade Towers. No human being could ever have been as amazed, as excited, as jubilant — and maybe as hysterical

— as were Jesus' disciples on that first Easter morning. Why should it surprise us that in their excitement about this divine event they made a mistake or two as they recalled the human events surrounding it? They were absolutely unanimous about one thing: Jesus died and came to life again. And would not any person be foolish to insist that if any inconsistencies crept into the details of the disciples' reports, we would not be able to trust that Jesus had risen at all?

While Lindsell's "battle" book was still blowing its ill wind into the faces of believers, we invited some of his field officers over to Fuller to tell us what they thought was wrong with us. Some came. And what they had to acknowledge to us was that we did not agree with their *theory* of what sort of book the Bible of necessity has to be. And, by implication, their theory of how God had to reveal himself to us.

I must admit that my distaste for fundamentalism comes from a deeper well than an intellectual disagreement about the Bible. I do not have the constitution a person needs in order to be a fundamentalist; the literalism and absolutism of fundamentalism run against the grain of my nature. I seem to have been born with a need to look at both sides of the question; fundamentalism is dead set against giving me permission to satisfy this need. I certainly know fundamentalists who display a richer grace and stronger love than I do. Their God is my God, their Savior is my Savior. And yet, I would not invite any of them to join me on a six-day fishing trip. I embrace fundamentalists as my brothers and sisters in faith, but we are not likely to become the closest of friends. ✢

CHAPTER TWENTY-THREE

The Unintentional Ethicist

When I arrived at Fuller in 1968, the teacher of Christian ethics was a man in his mid-thirties with the electric eyes of a recent convert, which he was — not from the world to Christ, but from Christ back to the world. Jaymes Morgan had the magnetic makings of a new breed of evangelical leader in a tumultuous time. But he had cancer, had had it for some months before I came on the scene, and he died hardly more than a year after I arrived.

Morgan's death left us with a big hole in the curriculum. I was by this time a tenured faculty member still learning how to teach the philosophy of religion — which deals with such things as how a powerful and good God could let the world get into the mess it seems always to be in. Now we needed someone to teach ethics — which deals with how weak and sinful human beings can know what is right and what is good. But evangelicals with scholarly credentials to teach ethics were rare at that time. We looked everywhere and found no one to match our needs. During one more futile meeting of our search committee, and after thinking about it for no longer than thirty seconds, I offered myself for the job. I proposed that we look for candidates in both the philosophy of religion and in ethics; if we found a philosopher before we found an ethicist, I would switch over to ethics. A generous offer, I thought; others were probably more impressed by my presumption!

The next thing we knew we had found a fine philosopher of religion, and there I was, at fifty, leaping into a complex and controversial subject for which I had few academic qualifications to recommend me. I did not have the time to make myself over into the sort of bona fide scholar who writes articles in academic journals and gives learned lectures at conferences. But I might be able, I thought, to teach future ministers how to guide their people through the moral quandaries of life.

When we talk about ethics in a theological seminary, we mean to be talking about what God requires of us and how we can know it. And since this memoir is, strictly speaking, about my walk with God and not about ethics, I will limit myself to three assumptions that I have made about God in our efforts to learn his will for the moral choices we are called on to make.

I assumed, first of all, that God the Father is the origin of all morality. If there were no God, there would be no morality, because nothing would be intrinsically right or wrong. Without God, we would probably create social conventions and social rules that might keep people from putting their hands on our purses or around our throats. But this is self-protection born of self-interest, and, while it may be practical, it does not have much to do with what is not morally right and morally wrong.

With God, we are called to act not in self-interest but in obedience to his moral law. The fact, however, is that obeying his moral law leads us to what is in the best interests of all of us. A rational God who would go to the trouble of creating a world full of free-willed people must, I thought, have a design in mind for how these people could best live together. God's design is what makes things right or wrong. We do right if we live according to his design. We do wrong when we violate his design. So what we call moral law — or the divine commandments — is a manual for life at its best.

Much of the time, if our hearts are pure, the commandments are all we need to live a good moral life. We know that when we talk, we must be truthful. When we make a promise, we must keep it. When we want something our neighbor has, we must keep our hands off of it. When our neighbor does us wrong, we must not kill him for revenge. And no matter how unhappy our marriages may be, we must be faithful to them. Thus, for most of our daily moral choices, we do not need to study ethics; all we need is a knowledge of God's commandments and a will to obey them.

But much of the time is not all of the time. No doubt corporate CEOs who lie to their shareholders and politicians who lie to their public know and believe intellectually that lying is immoral. Why then do they lie? They lie to others because they first lie to themselves. The lies we tell ourselves are the most subtle of all lies. Nobody wakes up in the morning and says to himself, "I think I shall lie to myself today." The deception happens in such a tiny fraction of a second that the self-deceiver is not even aware that he has lied to himself. What lies does he tell himself? One of them is the lie that *he* is not really lying when he tells a lie. Another is the lie that the moral law does not apply to him, at least not in this case. In short, people tell bold-faced lies about very important things, and feel no guilt about their lying because they lie to themselves about what they are doing. Their problem is not with their heads, but with their hearts.

My second assumption was about God the Son. I did not assume that Jesus Christ brought us a new ethic to replace the old one. I assumed that he showed us two new ways of understanding the old one. The first has to do with *what:* he showed us that if we have love, we will do *more* than just say no to what the commandments forbid. The second has to do with *how:* he showed us how to obey the moral law *in a way* that helps other people. Jesus' way of love, then, calls for doing *more* than saying no to bad things, and it is the way of doing good things in ways that are helpful to other people.

My third assumption was about God the Spirit. The Spirit of God is our eye-opener to the human situation that requires a decision from us. The moral law by itself is not enough to guide us. What we need is the ability to see what is really going on in the human circumstances to which we are trying to apply the moral law.

We must remember, however, that the Spirit is not like an eye surgeon; he does not remove our cataracts. Nor is the Spirit like an optometrist; he does not prescribe new lenses for our eyeglasses. The Spirit works on what lies behind our eyes. It is said that what we see lies eighty percent behind our eyes. It is that eighty percent that the Spirit works on.

Ordinarily, we see what we want to see. We do not see what we do not want to see. We do not want to see reality, because we are afraid of what it might tell us. The Spirit, however, gives us courage and honesty to want to see the truth no matter how much we fear it. This is how the Spirit opens our eyes to reality: he takes the blinders of fear away.

Seeing reality for what it is is what we call discernment. The work of discernment is very hard. Reality is always deucedly complicated; any human situation has far more to it than first meets anybody's eye. No one has twenty-twenty discernment. This is why we need other people to tell us what they see in the same chunk of reality that we are looking at. This is why people of the church need to share their visions of reality *with* each other before they shout their judgments *at* each other.

Teaching seminary students, I often used real-life situations about which someone had to make an important moral choice. Each student was given a written report of the situation. Invariably, some students protested: "Why do we need even to discuss it?" they said. "What is going on in this situation is perfectly obvious." But we did need to discuss it. Invariably, the students who thought that what was going on was as clear and as simple as the bark on a tree were shocked to learn that others, as smart and as spiritual as they were, were seeing things that they missed. It is always this way: discovering God's will *for* a human situation requires us to listen to what other people see *in* that situation.

I discovered a long time ago that listening to people who see reality differently than we do is one of the most important parts of discovering the will of God for that reality. Nobody sees reality whole; we all need others to show us the parts of it that they see better than we do. Nobody sees reality with total accuracy; we all need others to correct our own vision. This is why we need to pray for patience to see what is really going on *before* we decide what God wants us to do about it.

Consider what it was that opened Christian people's eyes to the fact that slavery was an evil thing. They had grown up listening to preachers who quoted passage after passage from the Bible to prove that slavery was not only the will of God, but was a blessing to both the slaves and their masters. What persuaded them that the preachers were wrong? What persuaded them that slavery was a curse to both masters and slaves?

It was not a scholar's new interpretation of Bible texts. The conversion came only when their eyes were finally opened to see slaves for what they were — members of the same human family as the masters who owned them, fellow human beings who, like them, wept when they grieved and laughed when they were happy, who aspired to better things for their children, and were as likely as any Calvinist to love the Lord their God. It took courage for people to see what they were afraid to see and hear what they did not want to hear.

During most of my years at Fuller Seminary I served on the Bioethics Committee of the Huntington Memorial Hospital, one of the larger hospitals in the Los Angeles area. The task of this committee is to advise physicians on the moral aspects of the life-and-death medical decisions they are called on to make. We had to begin with the facts of the case. The facts of any case, however, range well beyond the facts that the doctor writes on the patient's chart. The facts of the case include facts about the desires of the family of the patient, about the patient's religious beliefs, about the civil law, and about the likely consequences that a given course of action would have on still others.

Once a pediatric surgeon came to us with this problem. A woman who had recently arrived from mainland China, the mother of a three-year-old boy, was living in an apartment in Los Angeles while she waited for her husband to join her. She neither spoke nor understood English. One afternoon while she was talking to someone on the phone, her son toddled out of the apartment and went outside. When she put down the phone, she called to him but he did not answer. She rushed in panic to the recreational area where the swimming pool was. There she found her son lying face down in the pool.

The manager of the apartment called 911 and the boy was rushed to the hospital. His brain, the thinking part of it, was already dead, though he was still breathing. But there were other serious complications. The doctor called in a translator who relayed his words in Chinese to the mother. Here is the gist of what he told her: "Your little boy needs immediate surgery to stay alive. But if we do surgery and 'save' his 'life' he will exist on a respirator as a breathing vegetable for the rest of his life." He told the woman that she was the only person who could decide whether to operate or not.

But this woman did not have the slightest idea of how to go about making a decision; she had grown up in communist China and, as a woman, had never been allowed to make a major decision in all her life. She was paralyzed by the fear of her husband's wrath should he come home to a dead son. Through a translator, she told the doctor that she wanted him to decide what to do. He told her that he could not make the decision for her; only she could decide.

What was the right thing for the doctor to do? I did not know of a single biblical command that told me in so many words what God wanted him to do. What we needed was more than the divine law; we needed human wisdom. I remember that what we suggested for the doctor to consider (no ethics committee decides for a doctor) was this: we suggested that he tell the mother that he will do nothing for one week and that if she has no answer by then he would interpret her silence as a decision not to operate and to take her son off the respirator. I do not know what he did.

It is seldom enough that we know *what* we should do. We also need to sense *the right way* to do it. This is where love must do its work. Take our duty to tell the truth, for instance. Without love, we are likely to spout the truth with no regard for its effect on the person to whom we tell it. But if we have love, or empathy, we can put ourselves in the other person's shoes, and this will give us a better chance of seeing the right time and the right way to tell her the truth.

I cannot remember ever having told my children a lie. But I do remember times when I told them the truth at the wrong time and, what is worse, in the wrong way. And I know that telling them the truth at the wrong time and in the wrong way often hurt them worse than if I had told a merciful lie.

How do we know the right time and the right way to tell the truth? How do we know when and how to tell a person that she is dying, or that her son has gotten himself in jail, or that her husband has lost his job, or that she has made a fool of herself, or that her little child has an incurable disease, or that his wife is having an affair? What we need more than anything else is the Spirit of love to open our eyes and ears to see and hear what is really going on in the heart and mind of the person to whom we are talking.

I will briefly summarize what I have been saying about my view of God's role in our search for what is right and what is good.

- God the Father has shown us what is right and what is good in his design for the good life in his world.
- God the Son has shown us not a brand-new ethic, but a more excellent way of following the old one — the way of an unselfish love that nudges us to do *more* than the law demands and to do it always with a will *to be helpful* to other people.
- The Spirit of God opens our eyes to see and our ears to hear the conflicting and confusing voices of the human situation that requires a moral decision.

These three assumptions about God formed the backbone of my life as an ethicist. They seemed right when I began and they seem right to me still. ⚜

CHAPTER TWENTY-FOUR

God and I at the Writing Desk

I wrote several books during my years at Fuller, all of them after I had become fifty years old, but I never fancied myself to be an author. People like Philip Yancey and Madeleine L'Engle and Frederick Buechner are authors. Writing is their life and their livelihood. They do it enviably well, and I have envied them sinfully, but I am — or was — a teacher and preacher who, on the side, wrote some books.

I do share one thing with genuine authors: I love sentences. When I first heard Jacob Vandenbosch, my freshman composition teacher at Calvin College, tell us that the Lord loved sentences and that he cared about how we wrote them, I became a convert on the spot. Mostly, I love sentences that real writers write, but the trouble with loving other people's sentences is that the more I love their sentences, the harder it becomes for me to write my own. In fact, I do not like people for whom sentences come easy. I like writers who have to work so hard at sentences that they sometimes hate to sit down and write some more of them. Which is probably most writers. I once heard someone ask William Styron what it was like to write *Sophie's Choice,* and he said that it was like walking from Vladivostok to Madrid on his knees, and when I heard him, I felt his pain.

The first book I wrote was an answer to what is at once the most important and most practical question we can ask about God: How can God's appearance on earth as a human being two thousand years ago reach out over that great gap of time to transform a human life today? And change it in such a profound way that to describe it as a new birth is no exaggeration? I had in my doctoral dissertation been critical of the Anglo-Catholic and the Orthodox way of answering the question. But in an academic dissertation one need not provide the right answer to the question; one needs only to explain and criticize someone else's answer. I set out to provide and explore the apostle Paul's answer in a book called *All Things Made New,* later condensed and called *Union with Christ.*

The apostle Paul says that we are affected by the event of two millennia ago, but not by being united with the Christ who was there then. Indeed, Christ is no longer a historical figure from whom we are separated by the years. He has become the life-giving Spirit who connects us with Christ as if he were our contemporary. The Holy Spirit, or the Spirit of Christ, is the link between us. Therefore, when his Spirit gets into our spirits, it is really Christ who gets into our spirits. The great gap of time between Jesus and us is bridged by the Spirit.

While I was teaching ethics, it seemed right to write some books about morality and moral choices. One of them, the first, was called *Mere Morality*. I meant the word "mere" in *Mere Morality* to say three things. First, the word "mere" said that morality is mainly about ordinary life, not about heroic sacrificial works of love. Second, the word "mere" said that God's morality is a morality that all of us, no matter how separated we are by our faiths, can live by. And thirdly, it was "mere" morality because it has no saving grace for us when we do not violate it.

Though it is "mere" morality, it is the backbone of any human community. It calls us to the sort of life that fits God's rational design for human community. There will be and can be no genuine human community unless we can trust each other to tell the truth, trust each other to keep our covenants, trust each other to keep our hands off other people's property, and trust each other to hold our lives to be sacred. "Mere" morality, then, is the bedrock morality of any who want to live together in peace and harmony.

Another thing that writing *Mere Morality* impressed on me was that, clear and absolute as the moral law is, it does not tell us what we should do in *every* human situation. This is because we live in a world that bristles with moral conflict and is entangled in moral ambiguity. We can be caught in situations that almost require violating moral law, situations in which obedience to one commandment forces us to break another. Doris and I were in Amsterdam when the Dutch were still reliving the moral dilemmas they experienced while their country was occupied by the Germans. Tell the truth and you condemn Jews to death; tell a lie and you may save their lives. Christians told a lot of lies. Christians saved a lot of lives.

Then there was a little book with a long title that nobody ever remembers or can keep straight: *How Can It Be All Right When Everything Is All Wrong?* It was collection of sermons that Lois Curley — as fine a literary agent in her day as could be found — nudged me into publishing. She happened to have heard a summer series of sermons I had preached — sermons in which I had deeply in mind the early death of my friend Cal Bulthuis. Lois asked me for permission to submit the sermons to a publisher. I was skeptical, but, though I do not like writing, I do like being published, and so the book was born.

This plain little book taught me that what a writer experiences as he writes often has little likeness to what the reader experiences as she reads. I learned this when a woman called me out of the blue one Monday morning sounding, I thought, a little hysterical. She told me how she had been bred by her father to be a militant atheist and had on her own become a militant feminist. She told me that she had given a speech that weekend to 1,200 women in Seattle and that, as she walked off the platform, someone had stuffed a small book into her hands, which she in turn stuffed in her bag without thinking about what she was doing. Resting from the weekend the morning after on a lounge chair in her backyard, she put her hand into her bag for a Kleenex and pulled out the book. She said that she had read no more than a couple of chapters when she found God. Or God found her. She was not sure which. She asked God whether she would have to call him Father. And God said: "I do not care what you call me as long as I call you my child." It is true, God may be in the *writing* of a book; but what is even more important, he may also be in the *reading* of it. That little book told me that I was called to write books that were simple enough for my Aunt Sophie to read in bed and responsible enough for my colleagues to read with respect.

I also wrote a book called *Forgive and Forget*. The trade journal *Publisher's Weekly* described it as a "crossover" book. A "crossover" book is a bridge book that connects the academic and the ordinary reader just as it bridges the gap between Christian and secular readers. I had not consciously chosen to be a crossover writer, but it was not at all odd that I became one. I was a "bridge" sort of person, so it was natural for me to write "crossover" books.

When I was just beginning to work on this book, I looked for help from other people's studies of forgiving, but found virtually nothing. There were splendid theological books about being forgiven by God for the wrongs we have done against him, but there were almost none to help us forgive other people for wronging us. Today, a new book about forgiving is published practically every month. Several universities now have institutes where scholars can do empirical research into the effects of forgiveness. Scholars are writing dissertations about it. *Forgive and Forget* was a stone thrown into a pool, and it caused ripples that have never stopped.

Through the years since it was published, many readers have written to tell me that, in one way or another, *Forgive and Forget* saved their lives. Reading these letters has given me a new understanding of the healing power of God. God heals our guilt by forgiving it. We heal other people's guilt by forgiving them. And in the process, we get healed from the bitter poison in our memory of what they did to us. We can be healed by being forgiven and we can be healed by doing the forgiving. This is what I learned by writing, and close to a million people have learned by reading, this book.

I must tell you that readers' grateful responses, especially to *Forgive and Forget,* but to most all of my books, have helped me to open the door of my spirit to saving grace. They persuaded me that I was after all a person of genuine worth. And they persuaded me that my own feelings of unworthiness were neurotic distortions. I saw that those negative feelings did not come from spiritual insight, they came from psychological blindness. Far from opening the door to grace, they closed the door in its face. And I could not open the door to let grace in until I was first healed of the pathology that had locked it.

In this way, the worldly success of *Forgive and Forget* was one more eye-opener to the worthiness of my own self. And one more door-opener to the amazing grace of God. It seems ironic, I suppose, that my discovery of real worth in my spirit made it possible for me to see my real guilt and open my heart to real grace. I believe that my own experience is the experience of many; some people need to discover the loveliness of their own souls before they can discover the loveliness of God's grace.

I feel after every book I write as if it had been given to me as a sort of miracle. One time, when I was editing the proofs of a book I had just finished, I was seized by the mystery of how it had happened. How did a tangle of thoughts come together as a coherent paragraph? How did I happen to remember old experiences that illustrated an abstract point I was making? Where did the metaphors come from? The adjectives? The verbs? The adverbs? How does a good sentence happen? I had no idea. But I knew it could not happen without the grace of God, so I slid off my chair, fell to my knees, and, from my depths of delight, said thanks to him. ❖

CHAPTER TWENTY-FIVE

God and I, Almost Friends

When I finally retired from Fuller Seminary, people asked me what I planned to do with my time now that I would have a lot more of it to do things in. Sometimes I told them that I was going to develop a closer friendship with God. They usually chuckled. But I was serious. Abraham was God's friend. Jesus made friends of his disciples. In all honesty, I had never known God as a friend, not the way I know my other friends. Now, after seven years into retirement, God and I are still not what you would call close friends. What is taking us so long?

For one thing, good friends like each other and enjoy doing things with each other; cold hash with a friend is a lot better than fillet mignon with a stranger. But it has to be reciprocal. If I like you but you don't like me, we are not likely to be friends. So if God is to be my friend, he must like me, which is just what is hard to believe. For years — most of my life in fact — I have not found it easy to think that God could like me. Love me, yes, no problem; it is much easier to love unlovable people than it is to like unlikable people. To be liked, a person has to be likable and that's that.

Here is something else that makes it hard to be God's friend: He never, well, almost never, talks to me. From what they tell me, I gather that he talks to other people. Talks to them in the chummy sentiment of the Latvian spiritual:

My God and I go in the fields together;
We walk and talk as good friends should and do.

I walk and I talk, but God hardly ever says a word to me. He certainly talked to a lot of people in biblical times. He also talked to people like Martin Luther and Martin Luther King. Once a man, hopelessly delusional, told me that God had talked to him, told him that he was Jesus Christ, and that I had better address him with the respect he deserved or he might resort to force. But sane as I usually am, when I am with God, I do all the talking. Most of the time.

What is more, friends need to be pretty much of the same status. The rich and famous do not usually make close friends of the poor and unknown. If this is true, it would seem to cross us off God's list of friends before we've even thought about it. If there is anything we Calvinists under-stand, it is that God is too high and too holy for us to cozy up to as a pal; it is not easy for us to schmooze with the Maker of the Universe.

I once asked a friend of mine what he would do if he met

Jesus coming down the street. He said that he would run over to him, put his arms around his shoulders, and say: "Hi, old buddy, wonderful to see you." Then he asked me the same question, and I said that I would either fall on my face or run and hide. The Calvinist's kind of God is the one who appeared to Isaiah from his throne on high and caused the prophet to fall on his face and moan for his sins. Or the God of Sinai, high on top of the mountain, who told the Israelites that if they even touched the foot of the mountain, they would drop dead, a Calvinist's sort of God.

When Doris and I lived with Mrs. Ars in Oxford, we figured that since we would be living in close quarters with her, sharing her cramped kitchen and her outside toilet, we should become her friends. So we did the sorts of things younger friends do for older friends. Once, I tiptoed down to her basement when she was not home and pounded into manageable sizes the huge hunks of coal that the British burned in their fireplaces after the war. Doris swept the ashes out of her fireplace and washed her windows.

Mrs. Ars would have none of it. We were turning her world on its head She knew her place in the universe and expected that Doris and I would know ours. She and her late husband had spent fifty years in the service of the Oxford gentleman, and she knew that a gentleman's place is not in the cellar chopping coal down to size. Oxford gentlemen, male or female, were upstairs; the servants were downstairs. I tried to tell her that we were not gentlemen, we were Americans, but she knew better. And that was the end of it.

Mrs. Ars insisted that in her world gentlemen lived upstairs and their servants lived downstairs. Well, if I was the gentleman upstairs at Mrs. Ars's house, God is in the penthouse, on the 1,000th floor of the building where I live. Søren Kierkegaard taught us that God is "qualitatively and infinitely other" than we are. You just cannot get more unequal than infinitely. I do not think God was ever on Kierkegaard's list of close friends. Still, Jesus, the Son of God, called his disciples friends. And presumably he wants to call us friends too. I need to remember that this particular "upstairs Gentleman" came downstairs, and you cannot get further down than a cross.

Maybe the highest obstacle that, for far too long, kept me even from thinking about God — or Jesus — as my friend was this: good friends admire each other. They see admirable qualities of character in each other that they want for themselves. But the admiration has to be reciprocated. If I admire you but you have only contempt for me, I can forget about being your friend. But there is more: if you do admire me, I must believe that there is something in me that is worth your admiring; if I know that you admire me, but I cannot admire myself, we cannot be friends.

There is ever so much about God to admire and there is nothing about him not to admire. But is there anything about me that he can admire? As a child and for years beyond, I believed that there was nothing in me that anyone, certainly not God, could admire. Today, in my old age, I have begun to believe that I am someone whom God does admire. True, there is a lot of rubble in me that he does not admire at all, and a lot he has to forgive. But I believe — God help my unbelief — that he also admires me.

How did it happen that someone like me who despised himself so long now dares to believe that the Holy One finds qualities in him to admire? I will tell you one way it happened: God gave me the eyes to see myself through the eyes of some discerning friends. Let me introduce a few of them. Doris has been my longtime friend; she admires me and she has almost persuaded me that what she admires is the real me. All things considered, David Hubbard was one of the most admirable men I have ever known; his wish to be my friend made me believe that he admired me as well. Another man I admire very much is Max De Pree, a man as good as he is wise, which means that he is very good. He, too, simply by being my friend, has persuaded me that there must be something admirable in me. Still another friend whom I have admired for a long time is Neil Clark Warren; Neil was once a colleague at Fuller, but he stayed a close friend after he left. Simply by wanting to be my friend, Neil persuaded me that there were qualities in me that he can admire. These are people — and there are many more — who, on anybody's scale of values, are very rich in admirable qualities; if God does not admire them, I think he should take a second look. And if admirable persons like these see something in me to admire, I have to believe that God admires me too. If this were not true, Jesus would not have called me his friend.

I am still more comfortable kneeling before the Lord my Maker than I am looking him straight in the eye and calling him my friend. But I am well on the way to really believing that he wants to be my friend. Not instead of, but besides, being my Maker and Redeemer. This mustard seed of faith keeps me hobbling on shaky legs into a friendship with God. ✦

CHAPTER TWENTY-SIX

God and a Grateful Old Man

I f being eighty-one makes a person old, I have become an old man, and I must confess that when it comes to my walk with God, old age is a bit of a disappointment. Growing old has not brought me much closer to God or much wiser in his ways. I once thought that when I retired from a regular job and had no pressure to go here and there and do this and that, I would spend much more time with him. Hasn't happened. And I thought that, with more time to think about him, I would come to understand him better. Here, I think, I have made some progress — not much maybe, but enough to nudge me to work at it some more.

I have two main feelings toward God these days: gratitude and hope. Both feelings keep slipping in and out of my spirit, one on the heels of the other. When gratitude comes, hope is right behind. If I am feeling grateful to God for the gifts he has given me, I at once start hoping that he will give the poor of our world more gifts to be grateful for. I feel ashamed to feel so good with what I have while most people on our planet feel so bad about the little they have. And my shame makes me very impatient with God. Which is all right, because impatience is one of hope's life signs.

I learned long ago that if anything can be better than getting a gift, it is the gratitude we feel for getting it. There is no other pleasure to compare with it — not sex, not winning a lottery, not hearing lovely music, not seeing stunning mountain peaks, nothing. Gratitude beats them all. I have never met a grateful person who was an unhappy person. And, for that matter, I have never met a grateful person who was a bad person.

I know that, in one sense, there is a kind of duty to be grateful, but gratitude feels to me more like a reflex reaction to gifts that I am given than a virtue that I have labored to achieve. All we need to be grateful is the insight to recognize a real gift when we get one. A gift is not just something we get for nothing. Things we get for nothing can have a hook inside them — ask a bass who just bit into a free worm. I heard once of a wife who said that every time her husband gave her something unusually nice, she knew that he was bribing her to forgive him for something not so nice. Yes, things we get for nothing can have a hook in them, but a real gift is given only to give pleasure and comfort to the one who receives it.

Another thing I have learned about real gifts is that they always come with a person attached. My gift to someone always comes with an unwritten message: I want to be part of your life; take my gift, take me. And I know that when someone gives me a gift, she too is saying: I want to be in your life. And knowing that she is attached to it makes her gift doubly precious.

I do not understand how people can be thankful for a gift if they have no person to thank for giving it to them. We teach our children to say thank-you to their grandmother for her birthday gift; why should we not teach them to say thank-you to God for the gift of their birth? (This thought is a gift from G. K. Chesterton.) Why should we not teach them that every new dawn of every morning, every drop of rain, every budding tulip, every blade of grass, every lovely thought we think, every wonderful feeling we feel, every memory of pleasure past, every tingle of pleasure present, every touch of a loved one's finger, every hug from a laughing child, every note of a Mozart concerto, every coming home to our own place and people, every new hope that sees beyond a hard present — all of them are gifts with a Person attached.

When it comes to gratitude, we who are old have an advantage. We have more good gifts to remember and therefore more opportunities to be grateful for them. And we have stopped striving for things we do not have, which makes it easier for us to be grateful for the things we do have. The moment I say this, however, I am haunted by old people I know who can remember nothing or dream nothing. If I were God, I would fix the brain so that the older we get the clearer and more happy our memories — short-term and long-term — become. But I am not God, thank God, so I can only be grateful for the memories I have.

Some gifts are memories of what I was and reminders of what I have become. When I, an octogenarian with a weight problem, remember the scrawny kid that I once was, I feel grateful. When I remember my adolescent haplessness and then remind myself of how God nudged me into a creative life spent at the happiest work ever invented, I feel grateful. When I remember the times my spirit groveled under the belief that there were no redeeming features in me at all, no beauty, no virtue, no power, no loveliness in my soul that God could admire and find lovable, and then I recall how, gradually and in fits and starts, it was revealed to me that, along with my failures, my spirit was a treasury of lovable and admirable qualities. When I remember my boyhood sense that God had reprobated me to damnation and compare it with my old man's certainty that he has elected me to share his grace, I feel very grateful.

I remember how as a boy I dared not hope that any pretty girl would ever notice me, and the memory makes me grateful to be an old man with a wife so lovely I often stand and stare. I remember how superior men and women whom anyone would pray to be like crossed my path and then stayed as dear friends. I remember how I, not yet fifty, could not persuade myself that I could write a book worth anyone's reading and how, after fifty, I have written a shelf full of them. I remember how on two occasions I was given at best a long-shot chance at survival after a raft of blood clots attached themselves to my lungs, and here I am still lifting weights at a gym. I remember how Doris and I, on three different trips to an adoption agency, came home with three very different children who now, after "many a conflict and many a doubt," nurture a warm affection for the aging parents who made so many mistakes in bringing them up. With memories like these, gratitude comes as easily as my next breath.

I remember magnificent things and I remember little things, and I feel grateful for them both. I remember that Jesus died to do whatever needed doing to let the river of God's love sweep me to himself, and I also remember the Velcro that makes it easy to put on my sandals. I remember my mother's weary weeping after a long week's labor, and I remember the pleasure Doris and I had with our first garage-door opener. Big things, little things, it matters little as long as they were gifts with a person attached.

But, then, when I thank God for being so very generous to me, I seem to imply that he must be a stingy crank to many others. When I remember that a thousand times ten thousands are living out a thousand varieties of hell on earth, my joy feels self-centered and obscene to me. This is why, on my little island of blessing in this vast ocean of pain, my "thank-you" always has the blues. ✦

CHAPTER TWENTY-SEVEN

God and an Impatient Old Man

I said earlier that, as I have grown old, my feelings about God have tapered down to gratitude and hope. Gratitude is the pleasure of hope come true. Hope is the pain of gratitude postponed. Gratitude comes easy, on its own steam, whenever we know that someone has given us a real gift. Hope comes harder, sometimes with our backs against the wall, laden with doubts that what we hope for will ever come. Gratitude always feels good, as close to joy as any feeling can get. Hope can feel unbearable; when we passionately long for what we do not have and it is taking too long to come, we are restless as a farmer waiting for rain after an August without a drop.

Please don't misunderstand me. Any hope, no matter how thin it gets, is better than no hope at all. To lose all hope is to die, inside; on the outside you are a walking cadaver, no less dead for being on your feet. Still, even if having hope is one hundred percent better than not having it, living by hope can get awfully wearying.

I have in mind what the Bible calls a "living hope," the hope that waits for God to do what needs doing to make his world work right. I also hope that when I die the gates of heaven will open up to let my disrobed soul inside, but for the life of me, I cannot get myself to hope that my disrobing will happen soon. Neither am I hoping for Jesus to come back to fly us off to glory or to judgment while God puts a torch to his world. What I am hoping for is what the prophets called a new creation and the apostle Peter called a new heaven and earth where righteousness is at home, the very same world that so delighted God when it came fresh from his hands. My hope goes for broke.

C. S. Lewis said somewhere that when God comes back to earth it will be like having the author of a play called on stage after the final performance; the play is over, he takes his bow, the players leave, and the theater is swallowed in darkness. I do not much like his metaphor. I believe that the Author of the play will appear on stage not after the final performance, but before the first curtain rises. The players have been turning rehearsals into nasty fights about who gets the best lines and the prime spot on the billboard; the play has become a disaster, doomed before it gets off the ground. It is then that the Author shows up, his original script in hand and with the power to change self-seeking egos into self-giving artists. The theater is bathed in gentle light, the curtain rises, and the play begins a triumphant and endless run. Not the ending, but the new beginning — this is what I hope for.

Hope is a universal human experience, and whether we hope as believers or as unbelievers, it always comes as a blend of three psychological ingredients. The first ingredient is a *dream:* we can hope only if we have eyes to see — albeit through a glass darkly — what it would be like for us if we got what we hope for. The second is *desire:* we can hope only for what we want — want, indeed, with a passion. The third ingredient is *faith:* we can keep on hoping only so long as we keep on believing that our dream will come true and our heart's desire for it will be satisfied.

When it comes to hope that God will come and fix his world, I claim to have all three ingredients: a dream, a desire, and a faith. But my faith often comes laden with doubt.

First, then, the dream.

I dream of a world where no father will ever abuse his child and where no child will ever abuse his father.

I dream of a world in which no mother will ever watch her children go to bed hungry.

A world where nobody ever points a gun at another human being or aims a bomb at any city.

A world where no family is torn apart by mistrust or brutality.

Where no woman will ever be assaulted or insulted by a man.

I dream of a world where no father or mother will die of AIDS and leave their children orphans.

A world where no aging person is sucked into the nowhere of Alzheimer's disease and where no person ever dies alone.

A world where no tribe or race will ever make war on their brothers and sisters nor make slaves of strangers.

I dream of a world where all will be well with all who live on God's good creation and where all God's children of every race, color, and culture will know that his Kingdom has come and, knowing that, will join hands and voices to praise their great Creator and Redeemer.

I have the dream all right, and I have the *desire* to go with it. I recall Jacques Ellul's saying that if your guts do not ache for what you say you hope for, you are not really hoping for it at all. I meet his test; when I hope that God will come and fix his world, my guts ache like the guts of an old man with gallstones.

They ache for almost fifty thousand children of Los Angeles who are prisoners of the county's child welfare system. For children taken from their homes by a police officer because their "parents" abused or abandoned them, children deposited like criminals in a depressing county building with the smell of a jail, and then shunted into a nonstop shuffle from foster home to foster home where life may be as bad as it was in the "home" they were rescued from.

Then, when I multiply the Los Angeles kids by the number of large cities there are in our world, I know that there are millions more kids cemented inside the same horrific prison, and my ache gets worse. And when, besides, I add the forgotten children of Africa crying for mothers whom AIDS has buried, my ache has me groaning the moans of hope almost lost. Then with these children still in my mind, I see the shrunken bodies of little children starving because no drop of the rain that is supposed to fall on the just and unjust alike has fallen on their land. With all of these children on my mind, how can I not have an ache in my guts so bad that I feel like bawling: *My God, my God, why have you forsaken them?*

Dream? Yes, I have it. Desire? In spades. But *faith?* I am not so sure about faith. Sometimes I hang on to faith by my finger nails; when the dream of a new world of Jesus' peace and love is more than two thousand years old and still shows no clear sign of coming true, anybody's faith is bound to turn to doubt. And yet, if you asked me, I would tell you that I simply cannot give up my faith that Christ will come back some time and in some form to make the world work right again. Maybe I keep believing because I do not have the courage to live without hope, I cannot say for sure. If my hope feeds on my weakness, so be it. Whether I hope because I do not dare to stop hoping or because I have a faith too strong to be tempted to give it up tells me nothing about whether my dream will come true. But, weak as it may be, I do have faith and could not give it up even if keeping it proved only that I was a gullible dunce.

My problem with my faith is the same problem that early Christians had with their faith: Christ's apostles had

told them that he would come back soon and make everything new and good again. But he had not shown up and
nothing had been made new, let alone good. In their
doubts, they asked the apostle Peter for a good reason why
— in view of Jesus' failure to make an appearance — they
should keep believing that he would ever come back and fix
God's world. Peter had only one reason to offer them: God
promised. That was all there was to it. A promise. Trust the
promise, he said; all things are possible, only believe.

But Peter tried to reassure them with still another
thought. It was not as if God were loitering, stopping for
some sightseeing here and there, the apostle said; he waits
so that more people will have a chance to get saved before he
comes. I have news for the fisherman: we are getting so
many more people in our world so fast that if new babies
keep getting born at the present tempo, there will be millions more unsaved people when Jesus comes than there
were in Peter's day. To signal his return, Jesus said, there
will be earthquakes in diverse places. But there have been
earthquakes shaking the earth somewhere every second of
every hour of every day since he spoke. Jesus also said that
before he comes there will be wars and rumors of war. Well,
as I write, there are some forty-five wars going on in the
world and they are slaughtering both the just and the unjust.

"How many wars will it take, how much more butchery,
how much more blood, how much more mayhem, to get
you to move, Lord?"

One thing is for sure, if God does not come to fix his world, nobody else can do it for him. To be blunt about it, his is the only game in town.

I put all my eggs in God's basket for one reason: Jesus died and came back to life again. Then he became the life-giving Spirit to give us, be it in driblets, a sampling of the good world we are waiting for. This is where the trolley stops. If it could be proven beyond doubt that Jesus did not come alive after he was murdered, we have lost our one and only reason for hoping that there can be a good future for the world. Without Jesus we are stuck with two options: utopian illusion or deadly despair. I scorn illusion. I dread despair. So I put all my money on Jesus.

When I was young I hoped with all my heart that Christ would never come, that he would stay up in heaven where he belonged and leave me alone. Every Sunday morning as my family shuffled down to our pew in the Berean church, I was scared half to death by a biblical prayer, taken from the Book of Revelation, painted large on the front wall: *Maranatha; Even So Come Quickly, Lord Jesus.* I countered it, each Lord's Day, with a prayer of my own: *Oh, Jesus, please, take your time.* Now, when I am lying in bed awake at night, I find myself humming an impatient gospel song that chilled me to the bone every time the congregation sang it, always as if we were standing at the station waiting for a tardy train that is carrying our soldier boy back from the wars.

Oh, Lord Jesus, how long?
How long ere we shout the glad song:
Christ returneth, Halleluiah, Amen.

This is where I find myself now on the journey that God and I have been on, at the station called hope, the one that comes right after gratitude and somewhere not far from journey's end. It has been "God and I" the whole way. Not so much because he has always been pleasant company. Not because I could always feel his presence when I got up in the morning or when I was afraid to sleep at night. It was because he did not trust me to travel alone. Personally I liked the last miles of the journey better than the first. But, since I could not have the ending without first having the beginning, I thank God for getting me going and bringing me home. And sticking with me all the way. ✤

Coda

On December 19, 2002, my Dad, Lewis Smedes, met the train at the station called hope and arrived at his journey's end. He had completed his walk with God on this earth. My Mom, my brothers Charlie and John, and I miss him terribly. I imagine that the thousands of people who have been touched in some way by him miss him also. What helps me, and may help others, is to think about Dad with God. When Dad arrives in heaven, God walks up to him, smiles, stares into Dad's eyes, asks, "How are you?" and waits for Dad's answer — just as Dad had done to so many of us. God listens intently to Dad's answer. Then they are joined by old friends and colleagues: Cal, George, Henry, Harry, Jim, James, Shandor, Bill, and others. They sit with God. They ask questions and they receive answers. All the questions that Dad wrestled with — that we all wrestle with — start to have answers. What an incredible scene!

December 19 may have brought Dad to his earthly journey's end, but it also delivered him to a new platform, a new station, a new world. A new world where hope is no longer needed, where shame no longer exists, and where forgiveness is obsolete. A new world where joy abounds, grace merely defines movement, and peace is eternal.

— CATHY SMEDES